THE LEGAL OPERATIONS GUIDE TO ENTITY MANAGEMENT

Governance, Compliance, Records, and Lifecycle Management for Corporate Legal Teams

Iveliz Rivera

First Edition

Copyright, Publication Notice, and Professional Disclaimer

Copyright and Publication Notice

This publication is an independent professional resource. Company names, service-provider names, internal systems, confidential work product, proprietary procedures, transaction details, and personal contact information from prior professional environments have been intentionally omitted. Any organizations, transactions, workflows, scenarios, or examples are fictionalized, generalized, or presented as composites for education and training.

Legal and Professional Disclaimer

The author, Iveliz Rivera, is a paralegal and is not an attorney licensed to practice law. The author does not provide, offer, affirm, validate, or represent that this book provides legal advice, legal opinions, legal representation, or services reserved to licensed attorneys or other regulated professionals. The author does not establish attorney-client relationships, select legal strategies or remedies for readers, determine legal rights or liabilities, or make jurisdiction-specific legal conclusions through this publication.

This book is provided solely for general educational, informational, training, and operational-reference purposes. It does not constitute legal, tax, accounting, audit, investment, financial, insurance, employment, privacy, cybersecurity, regulatory, compliance, corporate-secretarial, or other professional advice. It is not an official filing instruction, legal determination, tax election, governance approval, regulatory interpretation, certification of compliance, or assurance that an entity, filing, record, process, or transaction is legally sufficient, valid, authorized, complete, or compliant.

Use or purchase of this publication does not create an attorney-client, paralegal-client, fiduciary, agency, consultant-client, or other confidential or professional-services relationship between the author and any reader, purchaser, employer, organization, or third party. The book does not replace supervision, review, approval, or advice from licensed counsel or other qualified professionals. Paralegals and other nonlawyers must work within the limits of their training, role, delegated authority, applicable supervision requirements, professional-responsibility rules, and laws governing the unauthorized practice of law.

Entity-management laws, filing requirements, tax rules, beneficial-ownership obligations, professional-entity restrictions, regulatory standards, agency forms, fees, deadlines, and accepted practices vary by jurisdiction and change over time. Every form, checklist, sample, workflow, decision matrix, and procedure must be independently verified and adapted to the applicable facts, governing documents, contracts, organizational policies, agency instructions, and current law. Readers should obtain advice from appropriately licensed legal counsel and qualified tax, accounting, finance, information-security, insurance, and regulatory professionals before acting or refraining from acting.

Although reasonable care has been taken in preparing this publication, the author makes no representation or warranty, express or implied, concerning accuracy, completeness, timeliness, legal sufficiency, merchantability, fitness for a particular purpose, or results obtained from use. To the fullest extent permitted by applicable law, the author disclaims liability for losses, claims, penalties, damages, delays, costs, errors, omissions, rejected filings, missed deadlines, compliance failures, or other consequences arising from use, misuse, interpretation, or reliance on this publication. Nothing in this disclaimer excludes or limits any right or liability that cannot lawfully be excluded or limited.

First Edition, 2026 | Printed in the United States of America

ISBN-13: 979-8-9973103-0-1

Dedication

To my daughters, who I hope will always see in me an example of dedication, determination, resilience, and hard work. May my journey remind you that success is built through perseverance, courage, and the willingness to keep moving forward even when the path is difficult.

To the mentors, colleagues, and professionals who have contributed to my growth and reinforced the importance of integrity, discipline, and excellence.

And to the legal operations professionals, corporate paralegals, governance specialists, compliance teams, and business partners whose work often happens behind the scenes but remains essential to every successful organization.

This book is dedicated to those who continue to learn, lead, improve systems, overcome challenges, and bring clarity and order to complex environments.

Preface

Entity management is often described as administrative work. That description misses its strategic importance. Every active legal entity creates a network of obligations: formation records, governing documents, tax registrations, annual filings, licenses, ownership data, authorities, contracts, bank accounts, registered-agent relationships, and records that must remain accurate through years of growth and change. When those obligations are managed well, the organization can move quickly. When they are neglected, routine transactions become expensive investigations.

This guide began as a practical operating manual: a set of steps for forming entities, requesting certificates, obtaining employer identification numbers, maintaining records, tracking annual filings, qualifying entities to do business in additional jurisdictions, supporting lien searches, drafting organizational documents, reconciling expenses, and closing entities that had reached the end of their useful life. Those procedures reflected the daily realities of entity management. They also revealed a broader truth: a checklist is valuable, but a mature program requires more than a list of tasks.

A legal operations professional must understand why the task exists, who has authority to approve it, what data must be captured, which systems should hold the official record, what evidence proves completion, what downstream teams rely on the information, and how the process can be audited. This book therefore expands the procedural foundation into a complete lifecycle framework.

The goal is not to turn every reader into a corporate lawyer or tax adviser. The goal is to help readers design and operate a reliable entity management function. The chapters focus on decision rights, workflows, controls, documentation, technology, vendor management, metrics, and practical governance. Legal concepts are explained in operational terms so that readers can recognize when a matter is routine, when it requires escalation, and how to prepare complete information for counsel and business stakeholders.

The audience includes in-house legal departments, corporate secretarial teams, legal operations professionals, corporate paralegals, compliance personnel, finance partners, private equity portfolio teams, project-development organizations, real estate groups, startups, nonprofits, and law firms supporting multi-entity clients. Some readers will manage five entities. Others will manage five hundred. The principles are the same:

establish a reliable source of truth, preserve evidence, assign ownership, meet deadlines, and make changes only through authorized processes.

The book is intentionally vendor-neutral. It does not depend on any particular registered-agent provider, entity management platform, cloud drive, e-signature system, or accounting application. Technology changes. Sound controls endure.

How to Use This Guide

The book is organized around the entity lifecycle. Parts I and II explain strategy, entity architecture, intake, formation, and organizational launch. Parts III and IV address the data, records, and compliance disciplines that keep entities healthy. Parts V and VI cover governance actions, ownership changes, transactions, due diligence, and wind-down. Part VII focuses on legal operations: vendors, budgets, metrics, technology, automation, training, and scale. Part VIII applies the framework through industry-based case studies. The final toolkit provides reusable forms, checklists, registers, and worksheets.

Readers building a new program should proceed in order. Readers inheriting an existing portfolio may begin with Chapter 27, "Entity Health Audits and Remediation," and then use the toolkit to document gaps. Readers preparing for financing, acquisition, or sale should focus on Chapters 34 through 40. Readers selecting a new technology platform should begin with Chapters 14 through 18 and 44 through 47 so that system design follows the operating model rather than replacing it.

Each chapter contains five recurring elements:

- **Operational objective:** the business result the process should produce.
- **Control points:** approvals, validations, and evidence that reduce risk.
- **Practice notes:** lessons that improve execution in real-world legal departments.
- **Common failure modes:** recurring mistakes and their consequences.
- **Implementation checklist:** practical steps for applying the chapter.

The templates are designed to be copied into an organization's preferred system. They intentionally avoid links, proprietary fields, and jurisdiction-specific legal conclusions. Before use, each template should be reviewed by appropriate counsel and adapted to the organization's policies.

Professional-Use Reminder

The author is a paralegal, not an attorney, and this guide does not provide or affirm legal advice, legal opinions, tax advice, regulatory interpretations, or professional services. Readers must not use any checklist, form, workflow, sample language, or operational recommendation as a substitute for current jurisdiction-specific review by licensed counsel or another properly qualified professional. Legal conclusions, tax elections, governance approvals, regulated filings, and decisions outside a user's delegated authority must be referred to the appropriate decision-maker. Users remain responsible for verifying current law, agency instructions, governing documents, organizational policies, and professional obligations before acting.

Quick-Start

Entity Management Assessment

Use this assessment to identify the program's most urgent priorities. Score each statement from 0 to 3:

- 0 - **Not established:** no consistent process or reliable record exists.
- 1 - **Informal:** the work depends on individual knowledge or disconnected files.
- 2 - **Defined:** a documented process exists but is not fully integrated or tested.
- 3 - **Controlled:** the process has clear ownership, evidence, monitoring, and periodic validation.

Control Area	Assessment Statement	Score
Portfolio inventory	We can identify every legal entity, its jurisdiction, type, status, owner, and business purpose.	
Source of truth	The organization has one authoritative entity register with defined field owners.	
Formation intake	New entities are formed only through documented business, legal, tax, and finance approval.	
Ownership	Ownership and capitalization records reconcile to executed legal documents.	
Authority	Directors, officers, managers, signers, and delegations are supported by current approvals.	
Minute books	Every entity has a complete, organized, and secure official record.	
Compliance calendar	Annual filings, taxes, licenses, and qualifications have assigned owners and lead times.	
Registered agent	Coverage reconciles to state records, and service of process has redundant routing.	
Data security	Sensitive tax, ownership, signature, and personal data are restricted and auditable.	
Transactions	Good standing, governance, ownership, and authority records can be produced promptly.	
Change control	Names, addresses, ownership, officers, and structural changes trigger cross-functional updates.	
Dissolution	Entities are closed through a documented wind-down rather than allowed to lapse.	
Vendor management	Vendor coverage, service levels, invoices, security, and export rights are reviewed.	

Control Area	Assessment Statement	Score
Metrics	Leadership receives meaningful reporting on risk, deadlines, quality, cost, and remediation.	
Continuity	Procedures, backup owners, and knowledge-transfer materials reduce dependence on individuals.	

Interpreting the Score

0 - 15: Immediate stabilization required. Focus first on service of process, filings due within ninety days, legal status, ownership, and access to core records. Do not begin a major technology implementation until the portfolio is inventoried and critical risks are controlled.

16 - 29: Reactive program. The organization completes many tasks, but the work is fragmented. Establish a master register, standardized intake, compliance calendar, digital minute-book taxonomy, and documented decision rights.

30 - 38: Defined program. Core processes exist, but integration and evidence may be inconsistent. Strengthen reconciliation, exception reporting, vendor controls, data history, audit testing, and transaction readiness.

39 - 45: Controlled program. The organization has a mature foundation. Focus on automation, predictive reporting, portfolio rationalization, system integration, and continuous improvement.

First Thirty-Day Priorities

Regardless of score, complete the following actions first:

1. Confirm that every service-of-process notice reaches a monitored legal channel with backup recipients.
2. Identify all filings, taxes, licenses, and renewals due within the next ninety days.
3. Produce an entity inventory and mark each record as verified, partially verified, or unverified.
4. Identify entities not in good standing, administratively dissolved, or carrying unresolved penalties.
5. Secure taxpayer identification numbers, ownership data, signatures, and personal identification records.
6. Identify active transactions, financings, audits, and disputes that depend on entity records.
7. Create a remediation log with risk, owner, deadline, and closure evidence.
8. Establish one intake channel for formations, changes, certificates, and dissolutions.

Maturity Roadmap

Stage	Primary Goal	Evidence of Progress
Stabilize	Protect deadlines, notices, and critical records	Ninety-day calendar, service protocol, verified inventory
Standardize	Make work repeatable	Approved SOPs, data dictionary, folder taxonomy, RACI
Integrate	Connect legal, tax, finance, licensing, and transactions	Shared triggers, reconciliations, linked records, dashboards
Automate	Reduce manual reentry and routine delay	Workflow, document generation, exception alerts, integrations
Optimize	Use data to reduce risk and cost	Rationalized portfolio, predictive metrics, tested controls

The assessment should be repeated after material acquisitions, reorganizations, system changes, or leadership transitions. A higher score is meaningful only when the supporting evidence can be produced and the controls operate consistently.

Contents

CONTENTS

continued

CONTENTS

continued

Introduction:

The Entity Lifecycle as an Operating System

An entity is not merely a record at a filing office. It is a legal and operational container. It may own assets, employ people, enter contracts, borrow money, hold licenses, receive revenue, incur liabilities, pay taxes, participate in litigation, and serve as a platform for investment or sale. The entity's value depends in part on whether the organization can prove what it is, who owns it, who controls it, what it is authorized to do, and whether it has satisfied its obligations.

Entity management is the discipline that keeps those answers accurate over time. It begins before formation, when the business decides why a new entity is needed. It continues through formation, tax registration, organizational actions, capitalization, licensing, foreign qualification, annual compliance, governance changes, financing, transactions, and eventual dissolution or divestiture. At every stage, the organization creates records that become evidence of authority and compliance.

The lifecycle can be understood as eight connected stages:

1. **Request and justification.** A business need is identified and documented.
2. **Approval and design.** Authorized stakeholders select the entity type, jurisdiction, ownership, governance, and purpose.
3. **Formation and onboarding.** Formation documents are filed, registrations are completed, and the entity is added to systems of record.
4. **Organizational launch.** Governing documents, initial consents, officer appointments, banking, insurance, tax, and licensing steps are completed.
5. **Maintenance and compliance.** Annual reports, taxes, renewals, registered-agent obligations, ownership records, and governance actions are tracked.
6. **Transaction support.** The entity is prepared for financing, diligence, acquisition, divestiture, or restructuring.
7. **Change and remediation.** Errors, delinquencies, governance gaps, data conflicts, and organizational changes are corrected.
8. **Exit and preservation.** The entity is sold, merged, converted, withdrawn, dissolved, or retained as inactive, and the final records are preserved.

A mature program treats each stage as part of one operating system. The master entity register, document repository, compliance calendar, governance workflow, vendor platform, and financial records must reconcile. No single spreadsheet or application can substitute for process ownership. The program succeeds when people know where to submit requests, who approves them, which record is authoritative, how deadlines are monitored, and what evidence closes each task.

This guide emphasizes three principles throughout. First, **the legal record and the operational record must agree**. Second, **authority should be documented before action, not reconstructed afterward**. Third, **a process is not complete until evidence is stored, data is updated, and downstream stakeholders are informed**.

PART I

ENTITY MANAGEMENT AS A LEGAL OPERATIONS DISCIPLINE

CHAPTER 1.

Entity Management as Legal Operations

The Operational Objective

The purpose of entity management is to preserve the organization's legal capacity to act. A well-managed entity can enter a transaction, open a bank account, demonstrate good standing, appoint an authorized signer, respond to service of process, and produce reliable ownership and governance records without an emergency search. The work is therefore not limited to filing annual reports. It is a legal operations function that connects corporate law, tax, finance, compliance, records management, technology, and business strategy.

From Task List to Control Environment

A task-based program asks whether a filing was submitted. A control-based program asks whether the filing was required, approved, accurate, timely, accepted, recorded, reconciled, and preserved. That distinction matters. A filing can be completed and still create risk if it uses the wrong address, identifies the wrong officer, conflicts with the governing documents, or is not reflected in the master register.

The strongest programs define a control objective for each recurring process. For example, the objective of an annual report process is not merely "file the annual report." It is to maintain the entity's authority to conduct business, ensure that public record information is accurate, avoid penalties, and preserve evidence of acceptance. The workflow should therefore include data validation, approval thresholds, deadline monitoring, payment confirmation, filing evidence, and system updates.

The Five Layers of the Program

A mature entity management function has five connected layers:

- **Governance:** decision rights, approvals, delegations, and escalation.
- **Process:** documented workflows, service levels, and handoffs.
- **Data:** accurate entity, ownership, authority, address, and deadline information.
- **Documents:** formation records, governing documents, consents, certificates, and evidence.

- **Technology:** systems that support intake, tracking, automation, reporting, and security.

Weakness in one layer affects the others. A sophisticated platform cannot correct unclear decision rights. A complete minute book cannot compensate for a missed foreign qualification. A detailed procedure cannot work if the data is unreliable.

The Entity Manager's Role

The entity manager acts as steward of the corporate record. The role may be held by a corporate paralegal, legal operations manager, corporate secretary, governance professional, attorney, or shared services team. Regardless of title, the core responsibilities are similar: manage intake, coordinate approvals, prepare and route filings, maintain the register and records, monitor obligations, support transactions, manage vendors, and report risk.

The role also requires disciplined escalation. Entity managers should not make unapproved legal or tax judgments. They should identify the decision, collect relevant facts, present options, document advice received, and execute the authorized course of action.

> ***Practice Note:*** *The most valuable entity managers do not merely answer, "Was it filed?" They can explain the entity's history, current status, authority structure, open obligations, and evidence supporting each conclusion.*

Common Failure Modes

Common failures include using multiple uncontrolled spreadsheets, relying on personal inboxes for deadlines, allowing business teams to form entities without legal intake, failing to record changes after filings, storing executed documents in project folders rather than the official minute book, and treating registered-agent notices as routine mail. Each failure creates a gap between the legal reality and the organization's understanding of that reality.

Implementation Checklist

- Define the legal department's ownership of entity data and records.
- Identify the official system of record for data and documents.
- Create an intake channel for new entities and changes.
- Establish approval requirements and escalation paths.
- Inventory recurring compliance obligations.
- Define evidence required to close each task.
- Implement monthly reconciliation among filings, documents, and the register.
- Report overdue items, data conflicts, and unresolved risks.

Key Takeaway

Entity management is an enterprise control system. Its quality is measured by the organization's ability to act with confidence, demonstrate authority, and produce reliable records when time and scrutiny are greatest.

CHAPTER 2.

Governance Roles and Decision Rights

Why Decision Rights Matter

Many entity management problems begin with an unanswered question: who is authorized to decide? A business leader may request a new company, finance may prefer a different ownership structure, tax may require a particular classification, and legal may identify regulatory or liability concerns. Without a defined approval model, the entity manager becomes the accidental decision-maker or the process stalls while stakeholders debate responsibility.

Decision rights should be documented for formation, dissolution, ownership changes, officer appointments, foreign qualification, registered-agent changes, tax elections, bank authority, and transactions. The required approver may be established by law, governing documents, board delegation, internal policy, financing agreements, or a combination of these sources.

The Governance Map

A governance map identifies both formal authority and operational responsibility. Formal authority may rest with a board, shareholder, member, manager, general partner, trustee, or authorized officer. Operational responsibility may rest with legal, tax, finance, treasury, human resources, development, or business operations. The map should distinguish four roles:

- **Decision owner:** the person or body with authority to approve.
- **Process owner:** the team responsible for completing and documenting the work.
- **Subject-matter reviewer:** the function that evaluates legal, tax, accounting, regulatory, or business implications.
- **Informed stakeholder:** the person or team that needs notice but does not approve.

A RACI matrix can help, but it should not replace governing documents. If an internal chart says the chief financial officer approves an action that the operating agreement reserves to members, the governing document controls.

Approval Tiers

Organizations often benefit from tiered approvals. Routine annual filings may be approved under standing authority. Administrative amendments may require legal and business confirmation. Formation, dissolution, ownership changes, guarantees, and material transactions may require governing-body approval. The approval matrix should also define monetary thresholds for expedited filing fees, vendor charges, penalties, and settlement of compliance issues.

Evidence of Authority

Authority should be captured in a durable record. An email may be sufficient for an internal routing decision but may not satisfy the legal requirements for an entity action. Formal actions may require a written consent, resolution, certificate, incumbency document, power of attorney, or amendment. The entity manager should understand the difference between an operational approval and the legal instrument that authorizes the act.

Escalation Design

An escalation path should address conflicting instructions, incomplete ownership information, urgent transactions, missed deadlines, service of process, suspected fraud, sanctions concerns, and requests to backdate documents. The process should protect the entity manager from being pressured to create a record that is inaccurate or misleading.

> ***Control Point:*** *No entity formation, dissolution, ownership change, or officer appointment should be treated as complete until the governing approval and the resulting legal record are both preserved.*

Implementation Checklist

- Inventory actions requiring board, shareholder, member, manager, or officer approval.
- Compare internal policies with governing documents and delegations.
- Create a RACI matrix for recurring entity processes.
- Define approval tiers and monetary thresholds.
- Establish an emergency escalation protocol.
- Require written evidence for material decisions.
- Review the matrix annually and after reorganizations.

Key Takeaway

A clear decision-rights framework prevents unauthorized action, reduces delay, and allows the entity manager to execute confidently without assuming legal or business authority that belongs elsewhere.

CHAPTER 3.

Entity Types and Organizational Architecture

Selecting the Right Legal Container

An entity structure should reflect the organization's purpose, ownership, tax strategy, governance needs, financing plan, liability profile, regulatory environment, and exit strategy. Legal operations does not choose the structure alone, but it must capture the decision and translate it into an accurate entity architecture.

Common structures include corporations, limited liability companies, limited partnerships, limited liability partnerships, professional entities, nonprofit corporations, trusts, and unincorporated arrangements. Each has different governance terminology, filing requirements, tax possibilities, and ownership records. A corporation typically has shareholders, directors, and officers. An LLC may have members and may be member-managed or manager-managed. A limited partnership has general and limited partners. The entity register should reflect the correct terminology rather than forcing every entity into a corporate template.

Parent, Subsidiary, and Affiliate Relationships

An organizational chart should show legal ownership, not merely business reporting lines. A business unit may report operationally to one executive while being legally owned by a different subsidiary. Confusing those concepts can result in contracts being signed by the wrong company, insurance being placed incorrectly, or assets being attributed to an entity that does not own them.

Ownership data should identify direct and ultimate parents, ownership percentages, classes or series of interests, and effective dates. Where ownership is held through nominees, trusts, partnerships, or joint ventures, the records should explain the chain sufficiently for authorized users to understand it.

Holding Companies and Special-Purpose Entities

Holding companies can separate investments, intellectual property, financing, or geographic operations. Special-purpose entities may isolate a project, asset, financing, or contractual risk. Their usefulness depends on disciplined separateness. If cash, contracts, employees, and records are mixed across entities, the structure may fail to deliver its intended operational or legal benefits.

Portfolio organizations should also define naming conventions. Names can reflect geography, project, investment sequence, asset type, or business line, but the convention should remain stable. A naming standard should prevent duplicate or misleading names and should account for state-specific restrictions and availability.

Joint Ventures

Joint ventures require special attention because ownership and control are divided. The entity manager should maintain the joint-venture agreement, governance thresholds, board appointment rights, transfer restrictions, deadlock procedures, capital-call provisions, and notice requirements. Routine actions may require approval from parties outside the organization.

Architecture as Data

The legal structure should be represented in more than a diagram. It should be stored as data that can be queried: owner, percentage, effective date, control rights, consolidation status, tax classification, and business purpose. Diagrams are useful for communication, but data supports reporting and reconciliation.

> ***Practice Note:*** *An organizational chart without effective dates is a snapshot with no history. Preserve prior versions and record when each ownership change became effective.*

Implementation Checklist

- Confirm the correct entity type and governance terminology.
- Document direct and ultimate ownership.
- Record management structure and control rights.
- Maintain effective-dated ownership history.
- Define naming conventions for portfolio entities.
- Distinguish legal ownership from operational reporting.
- Preserve joint-venture approval requirements.
- Reconcile diagrams with the master entity register.

Key Takeaway

Entity architecture is the legal map of the organization. It must be understandable, current, and supported by authoritative records.

CHAPTER 4.

Corporate Separateness and Risk Control

The Purpose of Separateness

Separate legal entities can help allocate ownership, assets, obligations, and risk. The protection is not automatic. Organizations must respect the distinctions among entities in their daily operations and records. Legal operations supports this discipline by ensuring that each entity acts in its own name, through authorized representatives, with appropriate approvals and documentation.

Operational Indicators of Separateness

Key indicators include separate formation and governing documents, accurate books and records, entity-specific bank accounts where appropriate, clear intercompany arrangements, correct contract parties, documented capital contributions and distributions, proper signatures, independent licenses, and compliance with required formalities. The exact requirements vary by entity type and jurisdiction, but the operational principle is consistent: records should show which entity acted and why it had authority.

Contracting in the Correct Name

Contracting errors are common and costly. A trade name may be used instead of the legal name. A parent may sign a contract intended for a subsidiary. A project company may be omitted from an agreement that concerns its assets. The entity manager can reduce this risk by maintaining a verified legal-name list, approved signature blocks, assumed-name records, and a contract intake control that confirms the contracting entity.

Intercompany Transactions

Shared services, cash management, employees, intellectual property, loans, guarantees, and cost allocations should be documented when required. Informal transfers may create tax, accounting, insolvency, or governance concerns. Legal operations should coordinate with tax and finance to ensure that intercompany agreements and approvals exist and are stored with the records of each affected entity.

Signature Authority

A title does not always establish authority. Signature authority may arise from bylaws, operating agreements, board resolutions, delegations, powers of attorney, or transaction-specific approvals. The program should maintain an authority matrix and expiration dates for limited delegations. When a signer leaves the organization, access and authority records should be reviewed promptly.

Warning Signs

Warning signs include invoices addressed to the wrong entity, bank accounts used interchangeably, missing intercompany agreements, inconsistent ownership records, unsigned governing documents, undated consents, contracts executed by former officers, and entities described as "inactive" while they continue to hold assets or obligations.

> ***Control Point:*** *Before a contract, financing, or asset transfer is completed, confirm the exact legal name, jurisdiction, entity number, authority of the signer, and required approvals.*

Implementation Checklist

- Publish verified legal names and signature blocks.
- Maintain an authority and delegation matrix.
- Review intercompany relationships with tax and finance.
- Require entity-specific documentation for material actions.
- Reconcile contracts, assets, licenses, and bank accounts to the correct entity.
- Remove former officers and signers from authority records.
- Escalate commingling or inaccurate-party concerns.

Key Takeaway

Corporate separateness is maintained through daily operational discipline. Entity management provides the records and controls that make the legal structure real in practice.

PART II

FORMATION AND ORGANIZATIONAL LAUNCH

CHAPTER 5.

Intake, Business Case, and Approval

Why Formation Should Begin with Intake

A new entity creates cost and continuing obligations. Before formation, the organization should understand the business purpose, proposed owner, anticipated activities, jurisdiction, timing, contracting needs, employees, assets, licenses, tax treatment, financing, and exit plan. A rushed request that says only "form an LLC today" is not enough to support a sound decision.

The Entity Request Form

A standardized request form should collect the information needed by legal, tax, finance, treasury, accounting, insurance, compliance, and the requesting business team. Core fields include proposed names, entity type, formation jurisdiction, principal business address, purpose, ownership, management structure, responsible business leader, requested completion date, reason for urgency, anticipated foreign qualifications, employee locations, regulated activities, bank-account needs, and expected contracts.

The request should identify whether the entity will hold real estate, intellectual property, licenses, debt, project assets, personal information, or other sensitive assets. It should also ask whether the entity is part of a financing or transaction with external deadlines.

Business Justification

The business case should explain why an existing entity cannot serve the purpose. Reasons may include risk isolation, investor requirements, tax planning, licensing, contractual obligations, local presence, asset ownership, project financing, or anticipated sale. The explanation helps prevent unnecessary entity proliferation.

Review and Approval Workflow

The workflow should route the request to appropriate reviewers. Tax may evaluate classification and elections. Finance may confirm consolidation and budget. Treasury may plan banking. Legal may assess entity type, governance, jurisdiction, and contracts. Compliance may identify licensing or beneficial-ownership implications. The business owner confirms operational facts and accepts responsibility for ongoing costs.

Urgency should not eliminate review. An expedited lane can shorten response times while preserving required approvals. The request should state the external deadline and consequences of delay.

Closing the Intake Stage

The intake stage closes when the organization has documented the approved entity design: legal name or naming strategy, type, jurisdiction, owner, management, purpose, registered-agent arrangement, responsible party for tax purposes, required formation documents, and target completion date.

> ***Practice Note:*** *A complete intake record becomes the formation file's roadmap. It also explains years later why the entity was created.*

Implementation Checklist

- Use one intake channel for all formation requests.
- Require a business purpose and requested completion date.
- Capture ownership, management, tax, licensing, and activity facts.
- Route the request to required reviewers.
- Document approvals and unresolved assumptions.
- Assign a unique request number.
- Preserve the final approved design with the entity record.

Key Takeaway

Formation begins with a business decision, not a filing. Strong intake prevents unnecessary entities, incomplete records, and downstream rework.

CHAPTER 6.

Choosing the Entity Type

A Multidisciplinary Decision

Entity type affects governance, ownership, taxation, financing, reporting, transferability, and liability. The choice should be made with legal and tax advice based on the facts. Legal operations supports the decision by collecting information, documenting the analysis, and ensuring that the chosen structure is implemented consistently.

Corporations

Corporations are commonly used when ownership is represented by shares, governance is divided among shareholders, directors, and officers, or investors expect a familiar capital structure. The program must track authorized and issued shares, classes, certificates or electronic records, director and officer actions, and shareholder approvals. A corporation's legal form does not determine its federal tax treatment in every case; tax elections require separate analysis.

Limited Liability Companies

LLCs offer flexible governance and economic arrangements. They may have one or multiple members and may be managed by members or managers. The operating agreement is central. Entity data should reflect members, managers, voting thresholds, classes or series, transfer restrictions, and tax classification. Using a generic single-member template for a complex LLC can create material gaps.

Partnerships and Limited Partnerships

Partnership structures may be used for investment funds, real estate, joint ventures, and other arrangements. The entity manager should distinguish general and limited partners, understand who has authority to bind the entity, and preserve admission, withdrawal, transfer, and capital records.

Professional and Regulated Entities

Professional corporations, professional LLCs, banking entities, insurance entities, healthcare organizations, and other regulated structures may have ownership, naming, licensing, or governance restrictions.

Formation should not proceed until the applicable requirements are confirmed.

Nonprofit Organizations

Nonprofit formation involves state-law organization and may also involve federal and state tax-exemption applications. The entity's purpose, governing documents, conflicts policy, board structure, charitable registrations, and restrictions on private benefit require specialized review.

Decision Factors

The analysis generally considers:

- identity and number of owners;
- investor expectations and transfer rights;
- management and voting structure;
- federal, state, and local tax treatment;
- employee and equity-compensation plans;
- financing and guarantee requirements;
- regulated activities;
- desired continuity and exit path;
- administrative cost and formality.

Documentation

The file should contain the approved recommendation or instruction, not merely the final filing. If tax classification differs from state-law form, the register should record both. For example, an LLC may be taxed as a partnership, corporation, or disregarded entity depending on ownership and elections.

> ***Control Point:*** *Never infer tax classification solely from the entity's state-law name or formation document.*

Implementation Checklist

- Collect ownership, governance, tax, financing, and regulatory facts.
- Obtain legal and tax approval.
- Record state-law type and tax classification separately.
- Select governing documents appropriate to the structure.
- Identify ongoing formalities and reporting obligations.
- Confirm that the master register supports the entity type's terminology.

Key Takeaway

Entity type is a design decision with long-term consequences. The entity manager's responsibility is to ensure that the approved design is accurately documented and maintained.

CHAPTER 7.

Selecting the Formation Jurisdiction

Home State or Another Jurisdiction

The formation jurisdiction may be the state of principal operations or another jurisdiction selected for legal, investor, financing, or administrative reasons. Forming outside the principal operating state can create a second layer of compliance because the entity may also need to qualify as a foreign entity where it conducts business.

Core Factors

The analysis should consider the location of operations, employees, real estate, customers, contracts, and regulated activities. It should also consider governing law, court system, filing costs, annual taxes, privacy rules, public disclosure, investor preferences, financing expectations, and the ease of obtaining certificates and completing transactions.

Cost of Dual Compliance

A common mistake is comparing only the initial filing fee. The true cost includes annual reports, franchise or privilege taxes, registered-agent fees, foreign qualification, local licenses, tax registrations, and administrative work. A low formation fee may not produce the lowest lifecycle cost.

Industry and Asset Considerations

Real-estate holding entities may be formed where the property is located. Project companies may be formed in a jurisdiction required by lenders or investors and then qualified where the project operates. Professional entities may be restricted to certain jurisdictions or ownership categories. Joint ventures may select a neutral or contractually specified jurisdiction.

International Considerations

Cross-border structures require specialized tax, sanctions, regulatory, and beneficial-ownership analysis. The entity manager should not rely on domestic formation assumptions when foreign owners, foreign subsidiaries, or non-U.S. activities are involved.

Decision Record

The formation file should contain the approved jurisdiction and the reasons or advice supporting it. This record is especially useful when a later team asks why the organization bears two sets of annual obligations.

> ***Practice Note:*** *The best jurisdiction is not necessarily the most famous one. It is the jurisdiction that fits the approved legal, tax, financing, and operational requirements.*

Implementation Checklist

- Identify the actual states of operation and asset location.
- Compare formation and recurring costs.
- Evaluate likely foreign qualifications.
- Confirm investor, lender, and contract requirements.
- Identify industry-specific restrictions.
- Obtain legal and tax approval.
- Preserve the jurisdiction decision in the formation file.

Key Takeaway

Jurisdiction selection is a lifecycle decision. Evaluate the full compliance footprint, not just the speed or cost of the initial filing.

CHAPTER 8.

Naming, Reservation, and Assumed Names

The Legal Name

The legal name must comply with the formation jurisdiction's rules and be distinguishable from existing names. It may need to include an entity identifier such as "Corporation," "Limited," "LLC," or an approved abbreviation. Certain words may be restricted or require regulatory approval.

Naming Workflow

A reliable process begins with several ranked name options. The entity manager searches the filing office's records, checks internal naming standards, identifies potential regulatory restrictions, and coordinates trademark or brand review when appropriate. A name-availability search is not the same as trademark clearance and does not guarantee the right to use the name commercially.

Reservations and Consents

If the organization is not ready to form, a name reservation may preserve availability for a limited period. Some jurisdictions permit use of a name that is otherwise unavailable with consent or other documentation. Expiration dates and renewal limits should be tracked.

Assumed, Fictitious, and Trade Names

An entity may operate under a name different from its legal name. These names may be called assumed names, fictitious names, trade names, or "doing business as" names. Requirements vary by state and locality. The entity manager should track the exact name, jurisdiction, filing office, registration number, effective date, expiration date, and associated legal entity.

Naming Conventions for Portfolios

Large portfolios need a standard that supports searching and reporting. A convention may include business line, geography, asset, sequence number, or project code. The standard should also address abbreviations, punctuation, state identifiers in internal folder names, and treatment of acquired entities whose names do not follow the convention.

Change Control

A legal name change affects more than the filing office. Contracts, tax records, bank accounts, licenses, insurance, payroll, websites, invoices, permits, and foreign qualifications may need updates. A name-change project should use a cross-functional checklist.

> ***Control Point:*** *Never treat name availability as trademark approval, and never treat a public-facing trade name as the legal contracting name unless the relationship is clearly disclosed.*

Implementation Checklist

- Obtain multiple proposed names.
- Confirm state-law naming requirements.
- Search availability and internal conflicts.
- Escalate regulated or sensitive words.
- Coordinate trademark review when needed.
- Track reservations and assumed-name expirations.
- Use verified legal names in contracts and records.

Key Takeaway

Naming is both a legal filing issue and a data-governance issue. A disciplined process avoids rejected filings, contracting errors, and portfolio confusion.

CHAPTER 9.

Formation Filings and Registered Agent Appointment

Preparing the Filing

Formation documents may be called articles, certificates, charters, or similar names. They usually include the legal name, entity type, registered-agent information, and other jurisdiction-specific information. Some states require a purpose, authorized shares, organizer, principal office, management structure, or initial report.

The filing should be prepared from the approved intake record. Before submission, verify spelling, punctuation, addresses, entity type, management designation, share authorization, organizer information, and requested effective date. An error in a public filing can affect contracts, tax registrations, or financing.

Effective Dates

Some filings become effective when accepted; others permit a delayed effective date. The desired date should be approved and coordinated with tax, accounting, and transaction timing. Do not assume that the submission date, acceptance date, and legal effective date are the same.

Registered Agent

The registered agent receives service of process and official notices. The agent must satisfy jurisdictional requirements and maintain a valid registered office. Organizations may use an individual, affiliate, law firm, or commercial provider. The selection should consider reliability, geographic coverage, notice-routing controls, security, reporting, and cost.

The registered-agent appointment should be recorded in the master register, along with the provider account, service address, renewal terms, and internal recipients for notices. Changes should be coordinated carefully so that no period exists without a valid agent.

Submission and Evidence

After filing, preserve the submission receipt, payment record, accepted formation document, filing number, effective date, and any initial report.

Update the entity register and create the official minute-book structure immediately. If a filing is rejected, record the reason and corrective action.

Expedited Service

Expedited service may be appropriate for a closing, contract, payroll, or licensing deadline. The request should state the business reason and obtain approval for additional fees. Expedite charges should not become a substitute for planning.

> ***Practice Note:*** *The entity does not become operationally ready merely because the state accepted the formation filing. Formation is the beginning of onboarding, not the end.*

Implementation Checklist

- Prepare the filing from approved source data.
- Verify legal name, type, addresses, agent, and governance details.
- Confirm the effective date.
- Obtain approval for expedited fees.
- Preserve submission and acceptance evidence.
- Record the entity number and effective date.
- Create the official entity record and trigger onboarding tasks.

Key Takeaway

Formation filings create the legal entity, but strong evidence and immediate system updates create a reliable operational record.

CHAPTER 10.

Employer Identification Numbers and Federal Tax Onboarding

Purpose of the EIN

An Employer Identification Number is a federal tax identification number assigned by the Internal Revenue Service. It may be needed for tax reporting, payroll, banking, licensing, and other business purposes. The EIN should be requested only after the legal entity is formed and the approved name and effective date are known, unless specific guidance supports another sequence.

Responsible Party

The EIN application requires identification of the responsible party. Current IRS instructions generally require an individual, rather than a nominee or formation service, for nongovernmental entities. The responsible party is the person who ultimately owns or controls the entity or exercises effective control over it, determined under the applicable instructions. Sensitive identifying information should be collected through a secure process and shared only with authorized personnel.

A change in responsible party or business address may require a separate IRS notification. The entity program should include a control for identifying these changes rather than assuming the original application remains accurate forever.

Completing the Application

The preparer should verify the legal name, trade name, mailing address, physical address, entity type, formation jurisdiction, formation date, reason for applying, principal activity, expected employees, and accounting year. Tax should confirm classification and any planned elections. A state-law LLC may have different federal tax classifications depending on ownership and elections.

Evidence and Security

Preserve the submitted application or internal intake, issuance confirmation, EIN, and IRS confirmation notice in a restricted location. The EIN is sensitive business information, and the responsible party's taxpayer identification number is highly sensitive personal information. Access should be role-based, encrypted, and auditable.

Downstream Notifications

Once obtained, the EIN may need to be provided to tax, accounting, payroll, treasury, banking, insurance, licensing, and transaction teams. The master entity register should store the EIN in a protected field, not in a broadly accessible spreadsheet.

> ***Control Point:*** *A formation agent, paralegal, or other nominee should not be listed as the responsible party merely because that person is processing the application.*

Implementation Checklist

- Confirm formation acceptance and legal effective date.
- Obtain tax approval for classification and application details.
- Identify the correct responsible party.
- Collect personal information securely.
- Preserve issuance evidence in a restricted repository.
- Update protected entity data.
- Trigger downstream tax, banking, payroll, and licensing tasks.
- Monitor future responsible-party and address changes.

Key Takeaway

EIN processing is a tax and data-security workflow, not a clerical add-on. Accuracy and controlled handling of sensitive information are essential.

CHAPTER 11.

Organizational Documents and Initial Actions

The Organizational Package

After formation, the entity needs internal rules and evidence of authority. The organizational package may include bylaws, an operating agreement, partnership agreement, initial board or member consent, incorporator action, officer appointments, manager appointments, share or membership issuances, fiscal-year decisions, bank resolutions, and approval of contracts or intercompany arrangements.

Governing Documents

Governing documents should match the entity type, ownership, management structure, and business purpose. A single-member LLC agreement may be concise, while a joint venture or investment entity may require detailed provisions on voting, transfers, capital, distributions, deadlock, and exit. Templates should be treated as controlled starting points, not automatic answers.

Initial Consents and Resolutions

Initial actions commonly adopt governing documents, appoint directors, managers, or officers, approve ownership issuances, authorize bank accounts, establish a fiscal year, approve tax elections, ratify formation actions, and authorize contracts. The entity manager should prepare an action list based on legal and tax instructions and route it through the correct approval process.

Execution and Dating

Documents should be dated consistently with formation and actual approval. Requests to backdate or create a false chronology should be escalated. Electronic signatures may be acceptable, subject to law, policy, and transaction requirements, but the final record should preserve complete signature evidence.

Minute Book Assembly

The final package should be assembled in the official minute book in chronological order. The entity register should be updated with directors, officers, managers, members, ownership, governance dates, and fiscal information. Any open items should remain on an onboarding checklist until resolved.

> ***Practice Note:*** *A state-stamped formation document proves the entity exists. It does not prove who currently has authority to act for it. That evidence usually comes from governing documents and organizational actions.*

Implementation Checklist

- Select the correct governing-document template.
- Confirm ownership and management structure.
- Prepare an initial action list.
- Obtain legal and tax review.
- Route documents for authorized execution.
- Preserve complete signature copies.
- Update authority and ownership data.
- Assemble the official minute book.

Key Takeaway

Organizational documents transform a newly formed shell into a governed legal entity with defined ownership and authority.

CHAPTER 12.

Ownership, Capitalization, and Authority Records

Ownership as a Controlled Record

Ownership records are among the most important and sensitive entity records. They support voting, distributions, tax reporting, beneficial-ownership analysis, financing, diligence, and sale. The organization should identify the authoritative ownership record for each entity type and restrict changes to an approved workflow.

Corporations

Corporate records may include authorized shares, issued shares, classes, par value, stock ledgers, certificates, transfer records, subscription agreements, and equity plans. The ledger should reconcile to board and shareholder approvals. Canceled certificates and lost-certificate affidavits should be preserved when applicable.

LLCs and Partnerships

LLC and partnership ownership may be reflected in governing documents, schedules, subscription agreements, contribution records, and transfer documents. Percentage interests may differ for voting, profits, losses, and distributions. The register should not reduce complex economic rights to a single unsupported percentage.

Capital Contributions and Distributions

Contributions may consist of cash, property, services, or other value, subject to law and governing documents. Finance and tax records should reconcile with legal approvals. Distributions should also be documented when approval is required. An unexplained cash transfer should not be treated as proof of ownership.

Authority Records

Authority data includes directors, officers, managers, authorized representatives, signing limits, and powers of attorney. Each appointment should have an effective date and supporting record. Terminations, resignations, and expirations should be recorded promptly.

Change Controls

No ownership or authority change should be entered solely from an informal request. The entity manager should require an executed transfer document, consent, resignation, appointment, or other supporting record and should confirm any conditions precedent.

> ***Control Point:*** *Ownership percentages, cap tables, and organization charts should reconcile to executed legal documents and approved transactions, not merely to financial assumptions.*

Implementation Checklist

- Define the authoritative ownership record by entity type.
- Record classes, percentages, and effective dates accurately.
- Reconcile legal and finance records.
- Preserve issuance, transfer, and cancellation evidence.
- Maintain an authority matrix with supporting documents.
- Restrict edit rights for ownership and authority fields.
- Review changes during quarterly or annual audits.

Key Takeaway

Ownership and authority data should be treated with the same control discipline as financial data because it determines who controls value and who can bind the entity.

CHAPTER 13.

Banking, Licensing, Insurance, and Operational Readiness

Formation Is Not Operational Readiness

A newly formed entity may exist legally but still be unable to operate. It may need a bank account, tax registrations, payroll setup, business licenses, insurance coverage, vendor onboarding, intercompany agreements, accounting codes, and system access. The legal team should coordinate a structured handoff rather than assuming other departments know that formation is complete.

Banking and Treasury

Banks may request formation documents, EIN evidence, governing documents, ownership information, beneficial-owner certifications, good-standing certificates, and resolutions identifying authorized signers. The entity manager should provide verified documents through secure channels and preserve the bank resolution and signer information.

Tax and Accounting Setup

Finance and tax may need to create general-ledger accounts, determine consolidation, establish tax calendars, register for state or local taxes, and document intercompany relationships. The entity record should identify the accounting owner and tax classification.

Licenses and Permits

Licensing obligations may arise at state, county, city, industry, or professional levels. Formation does not satisfy these obligations. The onboarding checklist should identify the activity, location, regulator, license owner, renewal date, and responsible business team.

Insurance

The organization should confirm whether the entity is covered under existing policies, requires endorsements, or needs entity-specific coverage. Assets, employees, project activities, and contractual requirements may affect the analysis. Evidence of coverage should be coordinated with the insurance or risk-management function.

Contract and Vendor Readiness

The business should use the verified legal name, approved signature block, notice address, tax forms, and payment instructions. Contract templates, procurement systems, and invoicing records should be updated to prevent the parent or another affiliate from becoming the unintended party.

Readiness Certificate

Some organizations use an internal readiness confirmation stating that required formation, tax, governance, banking, accounting, licensing, and insurance tasks are complete or identifying open conditions. This is especially useful for project companies and transaction-driven entities.

> ***Practice Note:*** *Assign each onboarding task to a named function and due date. A general email announcing formation rarely produces reliable completion.*

Implementation Checklist

- Notify tax, finance, treasury, accounting, insurance, and business owners.
- Establish banking and signer authority.
- Complete required tax registrations.
- Identify licenses and permits.
- Confirm insurance treatment.
- Update contract, procurement, and invoicing systems.
- Close or document every onboarding item.

Key Takeaway

Operational readiness is a cross-functional project. The entity manager coordinates the evidence that allows the entity to function as intended.

PART III

DATA, RECORDS, AND INFORMATION GOVERNANCE

CHAPTER 14.

The Master Entity Register

The Register as the Source of Truth

The master entity register is the structured record of the organization's legal entities. It should answer fundamental questions without requiring a search through email or folders: What is the exact legal name? Where and when was the entity formed? Is it active? Who owns and controls it? Where is it qualified? Who is the registered agent? What filings are due? Which documents prove the answers?

A register can be maintained in an entity management platform, database, or carefully controlled spreadsheet. The tool matters less than the governance. The organization must define who owns each field, who may edit it, how changes are approved, and how the data is reconciled to source documents.

Core Data Categories

A comprehensive register generally includes:

- legal name, prior names, trade names, and internal identifiers;
- entity type, jurisdiction, formation date, effective date, and filing number;
- current status and status date;
- principal, mailing, and registered-office addresses;
- registered agent and service dates;
- direct and ultimate ownership;
- directors, officers, managers, members, partners, and authorized signers;
- tax identifiers and classifications in restricted fields;
- foreign qualifications and withdrawals;
- annual-report, franchise-tax, and license deadlines;
- governing-document dates;
- business purpose, responsible business owner, and accounting owner;
- links or references to authoritative documents;
- transaction, financing, or project associations;
- dissolution, merger, sale, or conversion history.

Data Dictionary

Every field should have a definition, format, owner, source, and validation rule. For example, "status" may mean state record status, internal operational status, or both. If the term is not defined, teams may use "inactive" to describe an entity that still exists legally, holds assets, and owes annual taxes.

A data dictionary should also define permitted values. Free-text fields invite spelling variations and unreliable reporting. Use controlled lists for entity type, jurisdiction, status, tax classification, business line, and lifecycle stage.

Effective Dating and History

The register should preserve history rather than overwrite it. Ownership, officers, addresses, names, and status change over time. Effective dates allow the organization to answer transaction and audit questions accurately. A current snapshot without historical records may be insufficient for litigation, diligence, or tax inquiries.

Reconciliation

At least periodically, the register should be reconciled to filing-office records, registered-agent records, governing documents, tax records, financial systems, and organizational charts. Discrepancies should be assigned, investigated, and resolved with an audit trail.

> ***Control Point:*** *A field should not be updated merely because a change was requested. Update it when the change is legally effective and supported by evidence.*

Implementation Checklist

- Define the register's purpose and authoritative status.
- Create a data dictionary and controlled values.
- Restrict sensitive fields and edit permissions.
- Require source-document references for material fields.
- Preserve effective dates and history.
- Reconcile data on a defined schedule.
- Report missing, conflicting, and stale records.

Key Takeaway

The master entity register is not a contact list. It is a controlled legal dataset that supports governance, compliance, transactions, and enterprise reporting.

CHAPTER 15.

Digital Minute Books and Document Taxonomy

The Official Record

A digital minute book is the authoritative collection of an entity's organizational and governance records. It should allow an authorized reviewer to understand the entity's formation, governing rules, ownership, authority, material actions, and lifecycle history without searching unrelated project folders.

Recommended Structure

A practical taxonomy may include:

1. Formation and state filings
2. Governing documents
3. Initial organizational actions
4. Ownership and capitalization
5. Directors, officers, managers, and members
6. Written consents and meeting minutes
7. Tax and identification records
8. Foreign qualifications and assumed names
9. Annual reports, taxes, and good-standing evidence
10. Licenses and permits
11. Registered-agent and service-of-process records
12. Financing and transaction approvals
13. Intercompany agreements
14. Amendments, mergers, conversions, and reorganizations
15. Dissolution, withdrawal, or sale records
16. Historical and superseded documents

The taxonomy should be consistent across the portfolio while allowing specialized subfolders for particular entity types or industries.

Final Versus Working Documents

The minute book should contain final, executed, filed, or accepted records. Drafts, negotiation versions, and internal comments belong in a controlled working area. Mixing drafts with final records creates uncertainty. A clear naming convention should distinguish "draft," "approved," "executed," "filed," "accepted," "superseded," and "certified."

Chronology and Completeness

Within governance folders, documents should be ordered by effective date. Each action should include the final consent or minutes and relevant exhibits. If a resolution approves an agreement, the executed agreement or a clear cross-reference should be retained where policy permits.

Accessibility and Security

Access should be broad enough for authorized work but narrow enough to protect sensitive information. Taxpayer identification numbers, ownership records, personal data, board materials, and service-of-process documents may require separate permissions. The repository should support audit logs, version history, backup, and retention controls.

Closing the Record

After a filing or governance action, the process owner should confirm that the final document is stored, named correctly, searchable, and linked to the register. A task is not complete while the only executed copy remains in an email thread or e-signature platform.

> ***Practice Note:*** *Treat the minute book as if a lender, buyer, regulator, auditor, or court may review it on short notice. That mindset improves organization and evidence quality.*

Implementation Checklist

- Establish a standard folder taxonomy.
- Separate final records from working files.
- Use consistent document-status labels.
- Preserve complete signature and filing evidence.
- Apply role-based access to sensitive categories.
- Link documents to register records.
- Audit completeness at least annually.

Key Takeaway

A well-organized minute book converts scattered documents into reliable evidence of the entity's legal history and authority.

CHAPTER 16.

Data Quality, Naming, and Version Control

Why Small Errors Become Large Problems

Entity data is reused across filings, contracts, bank documents, tax returns, licenses, insurance, invoices, and transactions. A minor error in a legal name or effective date can propagate across systems. Data quality therefore requires preventive controls, not only cleanup after a transaction exposes inconsistencies.

Naming Standards

Document names should identify the entity, jurisdiction when useful, document type, effective or filing date, and status. A consistent pattern may be:

Legal Entity Name - Document Type - YYYY-MM-DD - Status

Examples include "North River Holdings LLC - Written Consent - 2026-03-15 - Executed" and "North River Holdings LLC - Annual Report - 2026-04-01 - Accepted." Avoid ambiguous labels such as "final final," "new version," or "signed copy."

Internal entity folders may include jurisdiction abbreviations for navigation, but the legal name itself should not be altered. If an entity is named "North River Holdings, LLC," the comma and suffix should be captured exactly where legal accuracy matters.

Version Control

Drafts should use controlled version numbers or dates. The repository should prevent simultaneous uncontrolled editing. Once executed, the final document should be locked or designated as the record copy. Superseded documents should remain available but clearly labeled and separated from current documents.

Validation Rules

Validation can include required fields, jurisdiction codes, date formats, entity-number patterns, duplicate-name checks, and cross-field logic. For example, an entity marked "dissolved" should not have an active annual-report task without explanation. A foreign qualification should identify both the domestic jurisdiction and the qualified jurisdiction.

Quality Review

High-risk data should receive a second review. This includes ownership, tax identifiers, governing-body composition, formation dates, entity numbers, and transaction authority. Periodic sampling can identify systemic errors without reviewing every field manually.

Change Logs

A change log should record what changed, previous value, new value, effective date, source document, requester, approver, and person who entered the change. This is particularly important when the platform does not preserve full field history.

> ***Control Point:*** *"Correct" means accurate, complete, current, supported, and consistently represented across systems.*

Implementation Checklist

- Adopt document and folder naming standards.
- Define version-status terminology.
- Configure required fields and validation rules.
- Use second review for high-risk data.
- Preserve source documents and change history.
- Run duplicate, stale-date, and cross-field exception reports.
- Train users to distinguish legal names from internal labels.

Key Takeaway

Data quality is created through standards, validation, and change control. It should not depend on one person's memory.

CHAPTER 17.

Sensitive Information and Cybersecurity

The Sensitive Data Within Entity Management

Entity records may contain taxpayer identification numbers, home addresses, signatures, ownership information, bank resolutions, account details, powers of attorney, personal identification, board materials, litigation notices, and transaction documents. A repository that is convenient but poorly secured can create legal, privacy, fraud, and reputational risk.

Data Classification

The organization should classify information by sensitivity and apply controls accordingly. A simple model may include public, internal, confidential, and restricted. Public formation records may be broadly accessible. EIN confirmation notices, beneficial-owner data, personal identifiers, and bank documents should be restricted.

Least Privilege

Access should be based on role and business need. Users should not receive portfolio-wide access merely because they need one certificate. Administrator privileges should be limited, reviewed, and separated from routine use. Departing employees and contractors should be removed promptly.

Secure Transmission

Sensitive information should not be sent through unsecured email or stored in personal folders. Use approved encrypted channels, secure portals, or controlled collaboration spaces. Passwords should never be placed in the same message as the protected file. Where possible, use system-level access controls rather than individual document passwords, which can be lost and are difficult to administer at scale.

Authentication and Audit

Multi-factor authentication, strong identity management, audit logs, backup, recovery, and security monitoring should be expected for systems holding entity records. The entity team should coordinate with information security during vendor selection and periodically review access and incident procedures.

Data Minimization

Collect only what is needed and retain it only as long as required. An entity system may need to record that an identification document was verified without storing a copy indefinitely. Sensitive personal data should not be duplicated across spreadsheets and shared drives.

Incident Response

The team should know how to report suspected unauthorized access, phishing, altered bank instructions, fraudulent formation requests, or compromise of service-of-process notices. Preserve evidence and involve information security, privacy, legal, and leadership according to the incident plan.

> ***Practice Note:*** *Convenience is not a sufficient reason to place sensitive ownership or tax information in a broadly shared register.*

Implementation Checklist

- Classify entity data and documents.
- Apply role-based access and least privilege.
- Require multi-factor authentication.
- Use secure transmission methods.
- Minimize storage of personal identifiers.
- Review access periodically and upon departure.
- Test backup, recovery, and incident escalation.

Key Takeaway

Entity management is also information governance. Security controls must reflect the sensitivity and transactional value of the records.

CHAPTER 18.

Records Retention, Legal Holds, and Audit Trails

Retention as a Governance Decision

Records should not be retained forever by accident or destroyed without authority. A records-retention schedule should identify categories, retention periods, legal or business rationale, responsible owner, and destruction process. Entity records often have long or permanent value because they prove existence, ownership, authority, and material actions.

Permanent or Long-Term Records

Formation documents, governing documents, ownership records, board and member actions, merger and dissolution records, and certain tax or property records commonly require permanent or extended retention. Routine correspondence, duplicate drafts, and administrative receipts may have shorter periods. The schedule should be reviewed by counsel and tax professionals and should account for statutes of limitation, regulatory requirements, contract obligations, and business needs.

Legal Holds

A legal hold suspends ordinary destruction when litigation, investigation, audit, or another preservation duty arises. Entity records related to the matter must be identified and preserved, including emails, drafts, data exports, and system logs. The entity team should be included in hold scoping when ownership, governance, transactions, or service of process are relevant.

Audit Trails

An audit trail should show who created, changed, approved, filed, accepted, and stored a record. Systems should preserve timestamps and user activity. When manual processes are used, a transaction log can provide equivalent evidence. Audit trails are especially important for ownership and authority changes.

Destruction Controls

Destruction should be documented, defensible, and suspended when holds apply. Sensitive records should be destroyed securely. Closing an entity or migrating a platform does not eliminate retention obligations.

System Migration

Before replacing a repository or entity platform, plan for export of documents, metadata, field history, audit logs, and permissions. Validate the migrated population. A successful migration is not measured only by the number of files copied; it is measured by whether records remain complete, searchable, linked, and trustworthy.

> ***Control Point:*** *Never delete records merely because an entity was sold or dissolved. Retention and access obligations may continue after the entity's active life ends.*

Implementation Checklist

- Create an approved retention schedule.
- Identify permanent and high-value entity records.
- Integrate entity systems into legal-hold procedures.
- Preserve audit trails and change history.
- Document secure destruction.
- Include retention in dissolution and divestiture plans.
- Validate records during system migrations.

Key Takeaway

Retention protects the organization's ability to prove what happened. It must be intentional, legally informed, and integrated with technology.

PART IV

ONGOING COMPLIANCE AND ENTITY HEALTH

CHAPTER 19.

Annual Reports, Franchise Taxes, and Renewals

The Recurring Compliance Cycle

Most active entities have recurring obligations in their formation and qualification jurisdictions. These may include annual or biennial reports, statements of information, franchise or privilege taxes, registered-agent renewals, business-license renewals, and other filings. Requirements vary by entity type and jurisdiction and should be verified against current official guidance.

Building the Obligation Record

For each obligation, record the jurisdiction, filing type, due-date rule, period covered, filing office, fee or tax owner, required data, approval process, evidence of acceptance, and consequences of noncompliance. Do not rely solely on a vendor reminder. The organization's own calendar should remain authoritative.

Data Validation

Before filing, validate legal name, entity number, addresses, registered agent, officers, directors, managers, members, business activity, and ownership information as required. Changes should be supported by internal records. If the public filing requires information that conflicts with the register, stop and resolve the discrepancy.

Tax Coordination

Some annual obligations are legal filings; others are tax filings. The entity team and tax team should agree on ownership and evidence. A state filing may be accepted while a franchise tax remains unpaid, leaving the entity not in good standing. Status should not be inferred from one receipt.

Workflow Statuses

Useful statuses include upcoming, data requested, under review, approved, submitted, rejected, accepted, paid, evidence stored, and closed. Color coding alone is insufficient unless the meaning is documented and accessible to all users.

Late or Rejected Filings

A missed or rejected filing should trigger prompt escalation. Determine penalties, cure steps, tax consequences, transaction impact, and whether reinstatement is required. Preserve the rejection and remediation evidence.

> ***Practice Note:*** *Close the task only after acceptance evidence is stored and the register and next due date are updated.*

Implementation Checklist

- Inventory recurring obligations by jurisdiction and entity type.
- Maintain an independent compliance calendar.
- Validate filing data before submission.
- Coordinate legal and tax payment responsibilities.
- Track submission, acceptance, and evidence separately.
- Escalate rejections and delinquencies immediately.
- Update the next cycle after completion.

Key Takeaway

Recurring compliance is a controlled cycle, not a reminder service. Reliable completion requires verified data, evidence, and reconciliation.

CHAPTER 20.

Compliance Calendars and Control Frameworks

Designing the Calendar

A compliance calendar should convert legal and regulatory obligations into assigned, monitored tasks. It should include due-date rules, internal lead times, dependencies, responsible owners, approvers, backup owners, fees, and evidence requirements. Calendar design should account for weekends, holidays, mail delays, signature availability, and transaction blackout periods.

Lead Times

Internal deadlines should precede legal deadlines. A common model begins data validation sixty to ninety days before a filing, obtains approvals thirty days before, and targets submission early enough to cure rejection. High-risk filings may require longer lead times.

Preventive and Detective Controls

Preventive controls reduce the likelihood of failure: required fields, automated reminders, approval workflows, and standardized checklists. Detective controls identify failure: overdue reports, status mismatches, missing evidence, and vendor reconciliation. Both are necessary.

Segregation of Duties

Where practical, the person preparing a high-risk filing should not be the sole reviewer and approver. Payment authorization may also require a separate control. Smaller teams can use documented peer review or periodic management sampling.

Dashboards and Escalation

A dashboard should show obligations due in the next thirty, sixty, and ninety days; overdue tasks; rejected filings; entities not in good standing; missing data; and unresolved ownership or authority issues. Escalation thresholds should be clear. An overdue annual report may require legal leadership notification; a service-of-process notice requires immediate escalation.

Calendar Governance

New entities, qualifications, licenses, mergers, and dissolutions must trigger calendar updates. A calendar that is not integrated with lifecycle changes becomes stale. At least annually, compare the calendar to the entity portfolio and official records.

> ***Control Point:*** *Every obligation should have one accountable owner, even when several functions contribute.*

Implementation Checklist

- Define internal deadlines and lead times.
- Assign primary and backup owners.
- Build preventive and detective controls.
- Separate preparation, approval, and payment where feasible.
- Create escalation thresholds.
- Integrate lifecycle changes with calendar updates.
- Perform annual completeness testing.

Key Takeaway

A compliance calendar is an operating control. It must assign ownership, create early warning, and produce evidence of completion.

CHAPTER 21.

Registered Agent and Service of Process Management

The Registered Agent Function

A registered agent receives official legal and governmental communications on behalf of an entity. The role is often treated as administrative, but a missed lawsuit, subpoena, garnishment, tax notice, or regulatory communication can create severe consequences. Registered-agent management therefore requires both vendor oversight and an internal response protocol.

Portfolio Coverage

The register should show the agent and registered office for every domestic and qualified jurisdiction. Coverage should be reconciled to vendor invoices and state records. Orphaned appointments can occur after acquisitions, name changes, conversions, or vendor transitions.

Service of Process Protocol

The protocol should define how notices are received, authenticated, time-stamped, classified, routed, acknowledged, tracked, and closed. Internal recipients may include litigation counsel, general counsel, risk management, human resources, tax, compliance, and business leadership depending on the document.

The first transmission should preserve the full document, envelope or delivery record, date and time received, entity served, jurisdiction, court or agency, response deadline, and sender. Receipt by the registered agent may start a legal deadline even if the internal recipient has not reviewed the document.

Escalation and Redundancy

Service-of-process notices should not depend on one inbox or person. Use monitored distribution lists, backup recipients, and escalation for unacknowledged notices. Test the process periodically. False or suspicious notices should be reviewed, but they should not be ignored.

Vendor Performance

Track delivery time, accuracy, portal availability, escalation quality, invoice accuracy, coverage, and record retention. Service-level failures should be documented and addressed. A transition to a new agent requires coordinated filings and confirmation in every jurisdiction.

> ***Practice Note:*** *A registered-agent portal is a transmission channel, not the legal department's final record repository.*

Implementation Checklist

- Reconcile agent appointments to state records.
- Maintain monitored internal recipients and backups.
- Time-stamp and classify every notice.
- Track response deadlines and acknowledgments.
- Preserve complete service evidence.
- Review vendor service levels and invoice coverage.
- Test the protocol at least annually.

Key Takeaway

Registered-agent management is a legal response system. Speed, accuracy, redundancy, and evidence are essential.

CHAPTER 22.

Foreign Qualification and Multistate Operations

Domestic and Foreign Status

An entity is domestic in its formation jurisdiction. It may be considered foreign in another state where it registers to conduct business. "Foreign" in this context generally means out-of-state, not necessarily non-U.S. The requirement to qualify depends on the jurisdiction's law and the entity's activities.

Activities That May Trigger Review

Potential triggers include maintaining an office or facility, employing personnel, owning or leasing real estate, performing recurring services, holding licenses, entering local contracts, operating a project, or conducting sustained business activity. Many statutes also identify activities that alone may not constitute doing business, such as maintaining bank accounts or defending litigation. The analysis is fact-specific and should be made by counsel.

Intake for Qualification Analysis

The request should identify the state, start date, physical presence, employees, property, contracts, customers, revenue, licenses, and duration of activity. It should also identify the entity's domestic status and whether a recent good-standing certificate is required.

Filing and Onboarding

Foreign qualification may require an application, certificate of existence or good standing, registered-agent appointment, assumed name, initial report, and fees. After acceptance, add the jurisdiction to the register, calendar recurring obligations, update tax and licensing teams, and preserve the evidence.

Consequences of Failure

Consequences vary and may include penalties, taxes, inability to maintain an action until cured, contract issues, or transaction delay. Failure to qualify does not necessarily invalidate all contracts, but the risk should be assessed promptly.

Withdrawal

When the entity ceases business in a state, it may need to withdraw formally. Stopping operations or terminating a lease does not automatically end annual obligations. Confirm tax clearance, final reports, license closure, and registered-agent termination requirements.

> ***Control Point:*** *A foreign-qualification decision should be based on actual activity and current law, not solely on where a contract is signed or a bank account is opened.*

Implementation Checklist

- Use a fact-based qualification questionnaire.
- Obtain counsel's determination.
- Confirm domestic good standing.
- Complete registration and agent appointment.
- Add recurring obligations to the calendar.
- Notify tax, payroll, licensing, and finance teams.
- Withdraw when operations truly cease.

Key Takeaway

Foreign qualification connects legal presence to actual business activity. The process requires coordinated legal, tax, payroll, and operational review.

CHAPTER 23.

Good Standing, Certified Copies, and Apostilles

Understanding the Documents

A certificate of good standing, status, existence, or authorization is an official statement from a filing office concerning an entity's current status under that office's records. Terminology and content vary. A certified copy is an official copy of a filed document authenticated by the issuing office. An apostille or authentication may be required when a public document will be used in another country.

Transaction Requests

Lenders, banks, investors, buyers, licensing agencies, and counterparties often request recent certificates and certified formation documents. The request should identify the entity, jurisdiction, document type, required recency, delivery format, deadline, and whether an apostille is needed.

Confirming Status Before Ordering

Before ordering, review the entity's status and open obligations. A certificate may be unavailable if reports or taxes are delinquent. Resolve the underlying issue rather than repeatedly ordering. Also confirm that the exact legal name and entity number match the transaction documents.

Certified Copies

Determine which filing is needed: original formation document, amendment, merger, conversion, name change, or complete filing history. A certified copy does not necessarily prove current good standing. Transactions may require both.

Apostilles and Authentications

The process depends on the destination country, document type, issuing authority, and applicable treaty framework. Some documents require notarization or county-level certification before state authentication. Build sufficient lead time and confirm requirements with counsel or the receiving party.

Recordkeeping

Preserve the order, payment, certificate, issue date, and purpose. Certificates can become stale for transaction purposes even though the underlying entity remains in good standing.

> ***Practice Note:*** *Ask what the receiving party actually needs. "Certificate" can refer to several different documents, and ordering the wrong one can jeopardize a closing deadline.*

Implementation Checklist

- Confirm document type and recency requirement.
- Verify entity status before ordering.
- Match legal name and entity number.
- Identify all amendments or historical filings needed.
- Confirm apostille or authentication requirements.
- Preserve the final official document and order evidence.

Key Takeaway

Official certificates are transaction evidence. Accuracy, recency, and clarity about the intended use are more important than the speed of ordering.

CHAPTER 24.

Licenses, Permits, and Business Registrations

Beyond Secretary of State Filings

An entity may be validly formed and in good standing yet lack authority to perform a regulated activity. Licenses and permits can be required by federal, state, county, city, professional, environmental, construction, healthcare, financial, transportation, or industry-specific authorities.

Building the License Inventory

For each license, record the issuing authority, license type, legal entity, trade name, location, activity, license number, issue date, expiration date, renewal lead time, responsible business owner, qualifying individual if any, bond or insurance requirements, and evidence location.

Ownership and Personnel Changes

Licenses may be affected by changes in ownership, officers, managers, qualifying professionals, addresses, or business activities. Entity-management workflows should therefore notify the licensing owner when a transaction or governance change occurs.

Renewal Controls

Renewals may require continuing education, background checks, financial statements, tax clearance, bonds, insurance certificates, inspections, or local approvals. The calendar should reflect dependencies, not just the final due date.

Central Versus Distributed Ownership

Legal operations may maintain the inventory while business units complete technical renewals. The responsibility model should be explicit. A decentralized license should still be visible in the enterprise register so that leadership can assess risk.

Closure and Transfer

When an entity is sold, dissolved, relocated, or stops an activity, licenses may need transfer, surrender, or cancellation. Failure to close licenses can create fees, reporting obligations, or confusion about continued operations.

> ***Control Point:*** *A license belongs to the named legal entity and activity. Do not assume it automatically covers affiliates, locations, or successor entities.*

Implementation Checklist

- Inventory licenses by entity, activity, and location.
- Assign legal and business owners.
- Track dependencies and renewal lead times.
- Integrate ownership and officer changes with license review.
- Preserve issuance and renewal evidence.
- Surrender or transfer licenses during exit events.

Key Takeaway

Licensing is part of entity health. A complete program connects legal status, operational activity, responsible personnel, and renewal evidence.

CHAPTER 25.

Corporate Practice of Medicine and Physician Practice Entity Registration

Scope, Currency, and Use of This Chapter

The corporate practice of medicine, commonly abbreviated CPOM, is the body of statutes, regulations, licensing-board rules, judicial decisions, attorney-general opinions, and enforcement principles that governs who may own, control, employ clinicians through, or receive the economic benefit of a medical practice. The phrase "CPOM states" is useful shorthand, but it is not a fixed or universally agreed list. Some jurisdictions have an express statutory prohibition. Others regulate professional-entity ownership, prohibit unlicensed interference with clinical judgment, restrict fee splitting, require a medical-board certificate, or impose facility-specific licensing that can be just as consequential as a traditional CPOM rule.

This chapter provides an operational framework for professionally licensed physicians and the legal operations teams that form, register, maintain, acquire, or wind down physician practice entities. It is designed as an issue-spotting and control guide, not a substitute for state-specific legal advice. Requirements can change through legislation, rulemaking, board guidance, enforcement, or judicial decisions. The discussion is current through June 2026, but every filing and transaction should be verified against then-current law and agency instructions before implementation.

Legal verification point: Never rely on a generic "CPOM state list" as the final legal conclusion. Confirm the individual physician license, entity form, ownership, governing documents, medical-board registration, facility license, billing model, and management arrangement for each state and each line of service.

Why CPOM Is an Entity-Management Discipline

CPOM compliance is often treated as a health-law question that begins and ends with physician ownership. In practice, it is an entity-management discipline because the legal conclusion must be translated into formation documents, share or membership records, officer appointments, governing agreements, board certificates, professional registrations, assumed-name permits, renewal calendars, organizational charts, management agreements, transaction approvals, and evidence that clinical authority remains with appropriately licensed professionals.

A practice can be validly formed with the Secretary of State and still be unauthorized to render medical services. A physician can hold an active individual license and still practice through an entity that lacks a required certificate or uses an impermissible ownership structure. A professional entity can remain in good standing while its physician owner has died, retired, moved, lost licensure, or transferred ownership in a manner that violates professional-entity law. Legal operations must therefore manage the physician, the entity, the activity, and the relationship among them as connected compliance objects.

The Four Regulatory Layers

A complete CPOM review evaluates four overlapping layers. A favorable answer at one layer does not resolve the others.

- Individual professional licensure. Each physician must hold the license, registration, controlled-substance authority, and any specialty credential required for the services performed in the patient's location, subject to limited statutory exceptions.
- Entity authority. The organization must use a permitted entity type, satisfy ownership and governance rules, register with the Secretary of State, and obtain any medical-board certificate, professional-firm registration, or fictitious-name authorization.
- Facility and service-line authority. The location or service may require a clinic, ambulatory surgery, laboratory, imaging, pharmacy, dispensing, pain-management, behavioral-health, home-health, telehealth, or other operational license.
- Financial and operational structure. Management fees, revenue-sharing, compensation, leases, staffing, marketing, payer enrollment, billing, and control rights must comply with CPOM, fee-splitting, anti-kickback, self-referral, false-claims, and professional-conduct rules.

The Two-Track Registration Model

Physician-practice launches should be managed through two synchronized workstreams. Track One establishes the physician's authority to practice. Track Two establishes the entity's authority to provide, bill for, and hold itself out as providing professional medical services. Neither track should be marked complete until dependencies are reconciled.

Track	Core requirement	Primary evidence
Physician authority	Active license in each patient-location state; renewal; prescribing and controlled-substance credentials; required training; supervision or delegation compliance.	Board verification, license certificate, renewal receipt, DEA/state credentials, credentialing file.
Entity authority	Permitted professional entity; compliant owners and managers; Secretary of State filing; foreign qualification; medical-board certificate or registration; trade-name approval.	Stamped formation/qualification documents, board certificate, professional registration, ownership ledger, assumed-name permit.
Operational authority	Facility and service-line licenses, NPI, payer enrollment, CLIA or imaging approvals, local permits, malpractice coverage.	Licenses, exemption certificates, enrollment notices, insurance declarations, inspection evidence.
Ongoing controls	Annual or periodic renewals, owner-license monitoring, change notices, registered agent, good standing, governance actions, document retention.	Compliance calendar, renewal confirmations, board minutes/consents, change logs, audit trail.

Professional Entity Forms and Ownership

States may permit a professional corporation, professional association, professional limited liability company, medical corporation, ordinary corporation under a statutory exception, nonprofit health organization, hospital affiliate, academic entity, governmental entity, or another specially authorized structure. The correct form depends on the state of formation, the state where services are rendered, the professions involved, and whether the entity will be domestic or foreign.

Ownership rules may address who may be a shareholder or member, whether all owners must hold the same professional license, whether specified allied health professionals may hold a minority interest, whether owners must be licensed in the state, whether directors and officers must be licensed, and how shares must be transferred following death, incapacity, retirement, disqualification, or license suspension. These rules belong in the operating agreement, bylaws, shareholder agreement, transfer restrictions, legend language, succession plan, and ownership register. They should not be left to an informal understanding.

Control point: Secretary of State acceptance is not proof that a physician-practice ownership structure is lawful. Many filing offices conduct only a ministerial review. Preserve the separate licensing-board approval, counsel memorandum, or other authority supporting the structure.

Clinical Independence and Reserved Powers

Even when a nonprofessional organization may employ physicians or contract with a physician practice, unlicensed persons generally may not exercise medical judgment. Governing documents and management agreements should identify decisions reserved to the physician-owned professional entity or its licensed governing body. The exact list is state-specific, but the following subjects normally require heightened protection:

- diagnosis, treatment, prescriptions, referrals, and standards of patient care;
- clinical protocols, quality assurance, peer review, utilization decisions, and patient-safety policies;
- selection, supervision, discipline, clinical scheduling, and termination of physicians and other licensed clinical personnel;
- scope-of-practice, supervision, and delegation determinations;
- content, custody, amendment, retention, access, and lawful release of medical records;
- clinical coding and documentation judgments, while allowing administrative billing support;
- professional-fee decisions where state law treats pricing or collection practices as part of professional judgment; and
- responses to licensing-board complaints, adverse events, malpractice matters, and mandatory reports.

The business organization may commonly manage nonclinical functions such as office space, equipment, information technology, human resources administration, bookkeeping, procurement, marketing support, and revenue-cycle administration. The agreement must nevertheless prevent those functions from becoming indirect control over clinical decisions. Budget authority, default remedies, veto rights, data access, and termination provisions should be reviewed for practical—not merely textual—control.

Management Services Organizations and the "Friendly Physician" Model

In strict CPOM jurisdictions, organizations often separate the physician-owned professional entity from a management services organization, or MSO. The physician entity employs or contracts with clinicians, holds clinical contracts and professional billing rights, owns or controls patient records as required by law, and retains clinical authority. The MSO provides administrative infrastructure under a written management services agreement.

This structure is not a safe harbor. A physician owner who holds title but lacks meaningful governance, economic rights, access to information, or authority may be viewed as a nominee. Stock-transfer restrictions, succession arrangements, proxy rights, security interests, management fees, long-term exclusivity, termination payments, bank-account controls, and restrictive covenants can collectively transfer de facto control to the MSO. Counsel should evaluate the full arrangement, including how it operates in practice.

Practice note: Do not describe a physician owner as "friendly" in formal records, instructions, or agreements. The physician owner must understand and exercise the duties imposed by professional-entity and medical-practice law. The objective is compliant division of clinical and administrative responsibility, not circumvention of licensure rules.

The Physician and Practice Registration Stack

The following registration stack should be evaluated for every new physician practice, acquisition, location, and service line. Not every item applies in every state, but every item should be affirmatively marked required, not required, pending, or completed.

- Individual physician license and periodic registration in each state where patients are located or services are deemed rendered.
- Professional entity formation or authority, including professional designator and purpose language.
- Foreign qualification and any licensing-board approval for an out-of-state professional entity.
- Medical-board certificate of registration, certificate of authorization, professional-firm filing, or ownership certification.
- Assumed-name, trade-name, fictitious-name, or board-issued practice-name permit.
- Federal Employer Identification Number and state tax accounts.
- National Provider Identifier for the individual physician and Type 2 NPI for the organization when applicable.
- Medicare, Medicaid, commercial payer, workers' compensation, and other payer enrollment tied to the correct entity and location.
- Drug Enforcement Administration registration and state controlled-substance registration where required.
- Facility or clinic license, certificate of exemption, and medical-director designation.
- Clinical laboratory certification or waiver, diagnostic imaging registration, radiation permits, pharmacy or dispensing registration, and durable-medical-equipment enrollment where applicable.
- Local business license, zoning, occupancy, fire, signage, and tax permits.
- Professional and general liability insurance that names the proper entity, locations, and covered clinicians.
- Business associate agreements, privacy notices, medical-record protocols, cybersecurity controls, and data-retention requirements.
- Telehealth registration, consent, disclosure, prescribing, and records requirements for each state served.

A Twelve-Step Launch Workflow

1. Define the clinical model. Identify specialties, services, locations, telehealth states, clinicians, payer strategy, prescribing, laboratory or

imaging functions, and whether the practice will employ or contract with professionals.

2. Create the state-by-state legal map. For each state, document the CPOM posture, permitted entity forms, owner and governing-body eligibility, board-registration sequence, facility licenses, foreign-entity rules, and renewal obligations.

3. Confirm physician eligibility. Verify license status, disciplinary restrictions, ownership eligibility, name, address, state residency if relevant, controlled-substance authority, and ability to serve as an officer, director, manager, or owner.

4. Approve the entity architecture. Prepare an organizational chart showing the professional entity, MSO, affiliates, locations, contracts, bank accounts, billing flows, and reserved clinical powers. Obtain health-law and tax approval before formation.

5. Clear the name. Confirm Secretary of State availability, professional designator requirements, licensing-board restrictions, assumed-name rules, trademark concerns, and consistency across payer and patient-facing materials.

6. Form or qualify the entity. File formation or foreign qualification documents in the required sequence. Some states require board approval before the Secretary of State filing; others require formation first and board registration second.

7. Execute governance documents. Adopt bylaws or an operating agreement, organizational consents, ownership issuances, transfer restrictions, succession provisions, clinical-reserved powers, banking authority, and conflict policies.

8. Complete board and facility registrations. Submit physician-license verifications, ownership schedules, formation records, applications, fees, insurance evidence, facility information, and responsible-person designations.

9. Establish provider identities. Obtain tax and provider identifiers; enroll the correct billing entity, clinicians, locations, and reassignment relationships with payers.

10. Validate management and financial flows. Review the management fee, bank controls, payroll, revenue-cycle workflow, leases, equipment, staffing, marketing, and data access for CPOM, fee-splitting, fraud-and-abuse, and clinical-independence risk.

11. Conduct a launch-readiness review. Do not treat formation as authority to open. Confirm every required license, registration, certificate,

insurance policy, enrollment, contract, inspection, and local permit is effective.

12. Activate ongoing compliance. Load renewals, owner-license monitoring, change-notice deadlines, board meetings, corporate filings, registered-agent obligations, and facility renewals into the compliance calendar.

High-Scrutiny State Profiles

The following profiles address jurisdictions that frequently require enhanced entity-management attention. They are operational summaries, not exhaustive legal opinions. The filing sequence, eligible owners, exceptions, and agency forms must be confirmed for the particular practice.

California

California applies a strong prohibition against the unlicensed corporate practice of medicine. A general corporation or ordinary limited liability company ordinarily should not render professional medical services. A physician practice commonly uses a California professional medical corporation formed under the professional corporation statutes. The ownership, director, and officer structure must satisfy California law, and clinical decisions must remain with California-licensed physicians. When the practice uses a name other than the physician's own qualifying name, a Medical Board fictitious-name permit may be required in addition to Secretary of State and county-level name filings. Legal operations should preserve the professional corporation filing, shareholder-license evidence, bylaws, stock records, organizational consents, fictitious-name permit, and current physician-license verifications.

New York

New York requires close coordination between the Education Department and the Department of State. A professional service corporation or professional limited liability company generally must obtain professional-entity approval or a certificate of authority from the Education Department before the organizational filing is accepted by the Department of State. Proposed owners, directors, officers, and professional employees must satisfy licensure and current-registration requirements. Foreign professional entities face additional requirements, and health-profession owners commonly must be licensed in both the home state and New York. Annual or periodic professional-entity statements and triennial professional registration should be tracked separately from ordinary corporate filings.

Texas

Texas recognizes a strong corporate-practice doctrine but contains multiple statutory structures and exceptions. Physician practices commonly operate through physician-owned professional associations or professional limited liability companies. Certain nonprofit health organizations require Texas Medical Board certification and ongoing notice of governance changes. Pain-management clinics and other regulated service lines may require separate registration. The ownership and management arrangement must preserve physician control of medical judgment, and the management-fee structure should receive specific fee-splitting and fraud-and-abuse review.

Illinois

Illinois physician practices may use a medical corporation, professional service corporation, or professional limited liability company, depending on the structure. Registration with the Illinois Department of Financial and Professional Regulation is distinct from the Secretary of State filing. Owners and governing persons must satisfy professional-license requirements, and changes in ownership, name, or status should be evaluated for both agencies. The launch checklist should include the applicable IDFPR business registration, physician-license verification, Secretary of State evidence, assumed-name review, and renewal or change filing requirements.

North Carolina

North Carolina requires professional corporations and professional limited liability companies practicing medicine to obtain a Certificate of Registration from the North Carolina Medical Board. Domestic and foreign professional entities use separate pathways. The entity name must match the name registered with the Medical Board and Secretary of State. Registration is renewed annually; failure to renew can suspend the professional entity's registration and certification. Ownership, purpose, and multi-profession arrangements should be reviewed under the Professional Corporation Act and Medical Board rules.

Arkansas

Arkansas medical corporations require a certificate of registration from the Arkansas State Medical Board as part of the entity-authorization process. Foreign medical corporations also require board-level evidence of authority and good standing. Legal operations should confirm the correct filing order, verify all physician owners and governing persons, preserve the board certificate with the formation or authority records, and calendar both corporate and medical-board renewals.

Minnesota

Minnesota's Professional Firms Act permits specified professional-firm structures and requires a professional firm to file required information with each licensing board having jurisdiction over the services before furnishing those services. For a physician practice, this includes the Minnesota Board of Medical Practice professional-firm filing. Governance documents must preserve licensed professional judgment, and changes in ownership, governance authority, professional services, or firm status should be evaluated for amended board filings.

West Virginia

West Virginia uses board certificates of authorization for medical corporations, with separate considerations for allopathic and osteopathic practice. The board authorization is coordinated with the Secretary of State filing. Professional limited liability companies are governed by additional professional-LLC provisions. The entity file should identify the responsible board, preserve the certificate, verify all professional owners, and track changes that may require updated authorization or notice.

Oregon

Oregon imposes physician ownership and control requirements on professional medical entities and contains detailed professional-corporation and professional-LLC provisions. Because Oregon law in this area has been subject to significant legislative activity, current effective dates and amendments must be checked before formation, acquisition, or MSO restructuring. Legal operations should verify eligible owners, voting control, directors and officers, clinical-reserved powers, transfer arrangements, and any statutory requirements applicable to management services organizations.

Rhode Island

Rhode Island professional service corporations generally require every officer, director, and shareholder to be licensed in the profession and employed by the corporation in that practice, subject to statutory exceptions. The corporation must also maintain professional liability insurance required by statute. The corporate record should include license evidence, employment status, ownership records, insurance declarations, and procedures for promptly addressing death, disability, retirement, or loss of licensure.

Florida

Florida is not typically treated as a universal, traditional CPOM-prohibition state, but the Health Care Clinic Act can be the controlling entity issue. A clinic that does not qualify for an exemption may require Agency for Health Care Administration licensure, a qualified medical or clinic director, inspections, financial responsibility, and change-of-ownership approval. Exemption certificates are not self-executing and generally require periodic renewal. The analysis must focus on ownership, payer billing, services, statutory exemptions, and the specific location—not merely the entity type.

Arizona

Arizona generally permits a licensed health professional to practice through or be employed by any form of business entity, subject to profession-specific exceptions and protections against interference with clinical judgment. This flexibility does not eliminate facility, service-line, records, disclosure, supervision, payer, or controlled-substance requirements. Legal operations should document why the selected entity is permitted and separately evaluate every regulated service and location.

Nationwide CPOM and Physician-Entity Issue-Spotting Matrix

This matrix is a screening tool for the fifty states and the District of Columbia. "High" means the jurisdiction commonly requires a professional entity, physician ownership or control, a licensing-board certificate, or similarly rigorous structural review. "Elevated" means statutes, board positions, judicial doctrine, professional-entity restrictions, or fee-splitting rules warrant state-specific counsel review before launch or acquisition. "Activity-specific" means a broad physician-ownership prohibition may not control every practice, but facility, service-line, billing, supervision, and professional-conduct rules remain material. The matrix does not replace a current legal memorandum.

States A–I

Jurisdicti on	Screening posture	Operational focus
Alabama	Activity-specific	Confirm physician licensure, professional-entity options, fee-splitting, facility licenses, and local business registrations.
Alaska	Activity-specific	Review professional corporation rules, individual licensure, facility/service-line licensing, and foreign qualification.
Arizona	Activity-specific	General business-form flexibility; preserve clinical judgment and check profession-, facility-, and records-specific registrations.
Arkansas	High	Medical Board certificate of registration for medical corporations; verify foreign corporation authority and licensed owners.

Jurisdiction	Screening posture	Operational focus
California	High	Use a compliant professional medical corporation or statutory exception; validate owners/control and obtain Board fictitious-name permit when required.
Colorado	Elevated	Evaluate professional-service entity law, employment structure, fee splitting, clinic/facility licensing, and clinical control.
Connecticut	Elevated	Confirm professional-service entity ownership, physician employment authority, facility licensing, and change-of-control requirements.
Delaware	Activity-specific	Professional entity may be appropriate; review home-state CPOM law, service-location law, facility licenses, and foreign qualification.
District of Columbia	Elevated	Review professional corporation/PLLC requirements, physician ownership/control, trade names, facility licensing, and board rules.
Florida	Activity-specific	Determine Health Care Clinic Act license or exemption; appoint qualified director and track biennial exemption/other renewals.
Georgia	Activity-specific	Review fee splitting, physician supervision, facility and pharmacy/dispensing rules, payer enrollment, and local permits.
Hawaii	Elevated	Confirm professional corporation/LLC ownership, physician licensure, facility authority, and foreign professional entity requirements.
Idaho	Activity-specific	Assess professional entity and naming rules, individual licensure, facility/service registrations, and fee arrangements.

States I–M

Jurisdiction	Screening posture	Operational focus
Illinois	High	Register applicable medical corporation, PSC, or PLLC with IDFPR and Secretary of State; verify licensed owners and governing persons.
Indiana	Activity-specific	Review professional corporation/LLC law, fee splitting, controlled-substance and facility licenses, and payer registrations.
Iowa	Elevated	Obtain state-specific CPOM analysis; confirm professional entity, physician control, board requirements, and facility licensing.
Kansas	Elevated	Review corporate-practice doctrine, professional association structure, licensed ownership, fee splitting, and facility authority.
Kentucky	Activity-specific	Confirm professional entity rules, physician license/renewal, facility and prescribing registrations, and management-fee compliance.
Louisiana	Elevated	Review medical-board positions, professional medical corporation rules, ownership/control, facility licensing, and fee splitting.
Maine	Activity-specific	Evaluate professional corporation/LLC options, physician licensing, clinic/service-line requirements, and foreign qualification.
Maryland	Elevated	Review professional service corporation/PLLC law, licensed ownership, fee splitting, facility authority, and payer enrollment.
Massachusetts	Elevated	Evaluate professional corporation structure, Board and Department of Public Health rules, clinic licensure, ownership, and clinical control.
Michigan	Activity-specific	Confirm professional entity options, physician licensing, facility registrations, fee splitting, and local/payer requirements.
Minnesota	High	File professional-firm information with the Board of Medical Practice before services; preserve licensed professional governance.
Mississippi	Activity-specific	Track physician license plus dispensing, pain-practice, controlled-substance, facility, and other service-specific registrations.
Missouri	Elevated	Obtain state-specific CPOM and professional entity analysis; verify licensed control, fee arrangements, and facility authority.

States M–P

Jurisdiction	Screening posture	Operational focus
Montana	Activity-specific	Review professional corporation/PLLC, physician licensure, facility/service registrations, and foreign qualification.
Nebraska	Elevated	Confirm professional corporation/LLC eligibility, licensed ownership/control, board or agency filings, and facility licensing.
Nevada	Elevated	Review professional entity ownership, physician licensing, clinic/facility permits, business licensing, and change-of-ownership rules.
New Hampshire	Activity-specific	Confirm professional entity and naming rules, physician license, facility registrations, and management-fee compliance.
New Jersey	High	Use an authorized professional practice structure; validate permitted licensed owners, governing persons, fee splitting, and facility approvals.
New Mexico	Elevated	Review professional corporation/LLC authority, physician ownership/control, board rules, facility licensing, and prescribing credentials.
New York	High	Obtain Education Department professional-entity approval before Department of State filing; track owner licensure and periodic statements.
North Carolina	High	Obtain Medical Board Certificate of Registration, including foreign entity approval, and renew professional entity annually.
North Dakota	Elevated	Review professional corporation/LLC and licensing-board requirements, licensed ownership, foreign authority, and facility licenses.
Ohio	Elevated	Evaluate corporate-practice doctrine and professional association/LLC rules; protect physician judgment and review fee splitting.
Oklahoma	High	Confirm Professional Entity Act certificate/board verification, licensed ownership and managers, Secretary of State filing, and renewals.
Oregon	High	Apply professional medical entity ownership/control rules and current MSO requirements; verify recent statutory amendments and effective dates.
Pennsylvania	Elevated	Review professional corporation/restricted professional company structure, physician control, fee splitting, and facility licensing.

States R–W

Jurisdiction	Screening posture	Operational focus
Rhode Island	High	Professional service corporation owners/officers/directors generally licensed and employed; maintain statutory liability insurance.
South Carolina	Activity-specific	Confirm professional entity, physician licensing, facility and pharmacy rules, fee arrangements, and local registrations.
South Dakota	Elevated	Review professional corporation/LLC and board certification requirements, licensed ownership, naming, and foreign authority.
Tennessee	Elevated	Obtain current CPOM analysis; verify professional entity ownership/control, medical-board rules, facility licenses, and fee splitting.
Texas	High	Use physician-controlled professional structure or statutory exception; certify nonprofit health organization and register regulated clinics when applicable.
Utah	Activity-specific	Review professional entity, physician license, facility/service registrations, fee splitting, and telehealth requirements.
Vermont	Activity-specific	Confirm professional corporation/LLC authority, physician licensure, facility registrations, and foreign qualification.
Virginia	Elevated	Review professional corporation/PLLC ownership and employment exceptions, clinical independence, facility licensing, and change notices.
Washington	Elevated	Evaluate professional service corporation/PLLC and common-law CPOM concerns; validate owners, clinical control, and facility licenses.

Jurisdicti on	Screening posture	Operational focus
West Virginia	High	Obtain applicable medical or osteopathic board certificate of authorization; coordinate Secretary of State and professional LLC requirements.
Wisconsin	Activity-specific	Review professional service entity, physician licensing, fee splitting, facility rules, and payer enrollment.
Wyoming	Activity-specific	Confirm professional entity and naming rules, physician license, facility/service-line registrations, and foreign qualification.

Foreign Professional Entities and Multistate Telemedicine

A physician practice formed in one state does not automatically have authority to provide medical services in another. The receiving state may require both foreign qualification with the Secretary of State and a separate professional-entity certificate from the medical board or professional licensing agency. Some states will not recognize a foreign entity unless its owners would be eligible to own a domestic professional entity. Others require owners to be licensed in both the formation state and the receiving state, or require the entity to add a professional designator to its name.

Telemedicine does not eliminate this analysis. The physician generally must be authorized in the state where the patient is located, subject to compact, consultation, emergency, episodic, or other statutory exceptions. The entity must also assess whether repeated telemedicine activity constitutes doing business, whether a telehealth registration is available, which entity should enroll with payers, where records are maintained, and whether prescribing or establishment-of-relationship rules differ from in-person practice.

Ownership and License Change Events

Professional entity compliance can change immediately when an owner's personal status changes. The entity-management system should treat the following as legal events, not routine human-resources updates:

- new owner, redemption, transfer, option, pledge, proxy, voting agreement, or beneficial ownership change;
- death, incapacity, retirement, resignation, bankruptcy, divorce-related transfer, or estate administration;
- license expiration, lapse, suspension, restriction, surrender, disciplinary order, or change in state registration;
- appointment or removal of an officer, director, manager, medical director, supervising physician, or clinical leader;
- change of entity name, assumed name, principal office, practice location, registered agent, or professional purpose;
- merger, conversion, domestication, sale, recapitalization, management-company change, or change of control;

- addition of a new profession, service line, laboratory, imaging modality, dispensing function, or telehealth state; and
- closure, patient-record transfer, payer termination, surrender of controlled-substance authority, or dissolution.

The workflow should identify the required approval, statutory cure period, replacement owner, transfer price methodology, notice deadline, agency filing, payer notice, insurance endorsement, and evidence of completion. Ownership succession should be designed before the triggering event occurs.

Management Agreement Review Checklist

- The physician entity retains exclusive authority over clinical decisions and licensed personnel.
- The MSO cannot direct diagnosis, treatment, prescriptions, referrals, peer review, or professional discipline.
- Management fees are commercially reasonable and reviewed for state fee-splitting and federal/state fraud-and-abuse risk.
- Banking controls permit administrative processing without transferring unlawful control of professional revenue.
- Budgets, purchasing thresholds, and default remedies do not allow the MSO to force unsafe or unlawful clinical decisions.
- Patient records, privacy obligations, access, retention, and transfer rights comply with professional and privacy law.
- Branding, advertising, call-center scripts, and patient communications identify the actual professional entity and clinicians as required.
- Stock-transfer, succession, security-interest, and continuity arrangements have current state-specific counsel approval.
- Termination provisions protect patient continuity, record access, payer obligations, and legally required notices.
- The documented division of authority matches actual operations, training, systems permissions, and escalation practices.

Acquisition and Investment Due Diligence

Acquiring or investing in a physician practice requires more than confirming good standing. The diligence team should reconstruct the legal authority under which the practice has operated and determine whether the proposed transaction changes that authority. At minimum, review:

- all formation, qualification, professional registration, fictitious-name, facility, laboratory, imaging, pharmacy, and controlled-substance records;
- current and historical ownership, stock or membership issuances, transfer restrictions, legends, options, pledges, proxies, and succession documents;
- licenses and disciplinary history of owners, directors, officers, managers, medical directors, supervising physicians, and key clinicians;

- governing documents, clinical-reserved powers, management services agreements, leases, staffing arrangements, marketing agreements, and revenue flows;
- commercial reasonableness and fee-splitting analysis for management, billing, marketing, space, equipment, and professional services;
- payer enrollment, NPIs, reassignment, credentialing, provider-based status, billing numbers, and change-of-ownership requirements;
- facility licenses, exemptions, inspections, plans of correction, complaints, board correspondence, malpractice claims, and mandatory reports;
- patient-record ownership, privacy/security controls, business associate agreements, record-retention plan, and cyber incidents;
- change-of-control approvals, successor owner eligibility, physician-owner continuity, closing sequence, and post-closing notice deadlines; and
- operations in every state, including telehealth, mobile services, temporary clinics, and services performed through contractors.

Transaction control point: Do not close based on a promise to "fix the physician entity later." If the transaction transfers ownership or de facto control in violation of professional-practice law, the defect may affect billing, contracts, licensure, enforceability, and professional discipline from the moment of closing.

Common Failure Modes

Secretary of State-only analysis. The practice is formed as an ordinary LLC because the filing portal accepts it, but the medical board or professional-entity statute does not authorize that structure.

Unlicensed owner or governing person. An investor, management company, trust, holding company, or unlicensed executive receives ownership or reserved powers that state law limits to licensed professionals.

Missing board certificate. The entity is formed but never receives the required medical-board registration, certificate of authorization, professional-firm filing, or annual renewal.

Improper practice name. The Secretary of State approves a name, but the medical board requires a separate fictitious-name permit or professional designator.

De facto MSO control. Contract rights, bank control, default remedies, budgets, or succession instruments allow the MSO to control the practice despite nominal physician ownership.

Ownership event not reported. A physician retires, dies, loses licensure, or transfers shares without timely redemption, replacement, board notice, payer notice, or facility change filing.

Facility license overlooked. The entity structure is compliant, but the clinic, laboratory, imaging service, dispensing activity, or pain practice operates without a license or valid exemption.

Payer identity mismatch. The entity on claims, contracts, NPI records, tax forms, and professional registrations is inconsistent, creating recoupment and false-claims risk.

Telemedicine expansion by marketing decision. Patients are accepted in a new state before physician licenses, entity authority, prescribing rules, payer enrollment, and tax/foreign qualification are reviewed.

Stale legal memorandum. The organization relies on an old fifty-state survey despite legislative, board, or enforcement changes.

CPOM Master Register: Recommended Data Fields

- legal entity name, state of formation, entity type, professional purpose, and tax classification;
- each service state, foreign qualification number, medical-board certificate number, and renewal date;
- owners, percentage interests, license type, license number, issuing state, status, and expiration/registration date;
- officers, directors, managers, medical director, supervising physician, and governing authority;
- professional and assumed names, board permits, locations, service lines, facility licenses, and exemptions;
- individual and organizational NPIs, payer enrollment identifiers, DEA/state controlled-substance registrations, and CLIA numbers;
- MSO name, management agreement date, fee structure, legal opinion date, and reserved-powers version;
- professional liability insurer, policy number, limits, covered entities, and expiration;
- next renewal, owner-license monitoring date, change-notice deadlines, responsible owner, and reviewer; and
- links to official evidence, approvals, counsel memoranda, organizational charts, and signed governance documents.

Implementation Checklist

- Adopt a written CPOM intake questionnaire for every physician-practice formation, acquisition, and new state.
- Require a state-specific legal conclusion before selecting the entity type or ownership model.
- Map individual physician licensure and entity authority as separate but linked requirements.
- Confirm the filing sequence among the licensing board, Secretary of State, facility regulator, and payer.
- Build clinical-reserved powers and professional ownership restrictions into governing documents.
- Create a succession and disqualification process for every physician owner.

- Maintain a state-by-state registration and renewal calendar, including annual board certificates.
- Monitor owner and governing-person licenses, not only employed clinician licenses.
- Review management agreements, bank controls, data access, and actual operations for de facto control.
- Require CPOM review before ownership changes, mergers, conversions, MSO changes, new service lines, or telehealth expansion.
- Preserve evidence of legal review, registrations, licenses, renewals, change filings, and board approvals.
- Revalidate the nationwide matrix at least annually and whenever a state changes relevant law or guidance.

Selected Authorities for Current Verification

The following authorities are starting points for counsel and legal operations. They are included without hyperlinks so the reader must retrieve the current official text and agency instructions.

- California Business and Professions Code sections 2285, 2400, 2406, and 2415; California Corporations Code sections 13400 et seq.; Medical Board of California corporate-practice and fictitious-name guidance.
- New York Business Corporation Law Articles 15 and 15-A; New York Education Law sections 6507 and 6512; New York Limited Liability Company Law Article 12; New York State Education Department professional-entity instructions.
- Texas Occupations Code Chapter 162; Texas Business Organizations Code Chapter 301; Texas Medical Board nonprofit health organization and clinic registration materials.
- Illinois Medical Corporation Act, Professional Service Corporation Act, and Professional Limited Liability Company Act; Illinois Department of Financial and Professional Regulation business-registration materials.
- North Carolina General Statutes Chapter 55B, including section 55B-13; North Carolina Medical Board corporation and PLLC registration materials.
- Arkansas Code provisions governing medical corporations; Arkansas State Medical Board medical corporation applications and renewal instructions.
- Minnesota Statutes Chapter 319B; Minnesota Board of Medical Practice professional-firm registration materials.
- West Virginia Code sections 30-3-15, 30-14-9A, and 31B-13-1301 et seq.; applicable Board of Medicine and Board of Osteopathic Medicine materials.
- Oregon Revised Statutes Chapters 58, 63, 676, and 677, including professional medical entity and management-organization provisions; current session laws and effective dates.
- Rhode Island General Laws sections 7-5.1-1 et seq., including ownership, governance, and insurance requirements.
- Florida Statutes sections 400.9905 through 400.995; Florida Agency for Health Care Administration health care clinic licensure and exemption materials.
- Arizona Revised Statutes section 32-3230.01 and profession-specific business-entity, facility, and records provisions.

Key Takeaway

CPOM compliance is not a one-time ownership opinion. It is a lifecycle control system connecting professionally licensed physicians, permitted entity forms, governing authority, medical-board and facility registrations, management arrangements, payer identities, and change-event monitoring. The strongest legal operations programs treat every state, owner, registration, and clinical service as a documented dependency—and they verify those dependencies before the practice begins, expands, changes hands, or closes.

CHAPTER 26.

Beneficial Ownership and Federal Reporting

A Rapidly Changing Area

Beneficial-ownership reporting requirements have changed significantly and may continue to change. As of this edition, current federal guidance generally exempts entities created in the United States and U.S. persons from federal beneficial-ownership reporting under the Corporate Transparency Act, while certain entities formed under foreign law and registered to do business in the United States may remain subject to reporting. Organizations must verify the current rule before making a filing decision.

Broader Beneficial-Ownership Obligations

Federal reporting is only one context. Banks, lenders, investors, sanctions programs, anti-money-laundering controls, licensing authorities, tax authorities, and transaction counterparties may require ownership and control information. The organization should maintain accurate ownership data even when a particular filing obligation does not apply.

Decision Framework

For each entity, determine:

- whether it was created under U.S. or foreign law;
- whether it is registered to do business in a U.S. jurisdiction;
- whether a current exemption applies;
- whether non-U.S. ownership or control creates special requirements;
- which individuals or entities must be reported in a particular context;
- what change events require review;
- what evidence supports the conclusion.

Data Governance

Beneficial-owner information is sensitive. Use restricted access, secure collection, clear retention rules, and documented consent or notice where required. Do not place personal identification documents in a broadly accessible entity folder.

Change Monitoring

Ownership transfers, control changes, reorganizations, conversions, mergers, officer changes, and address changes may affect reporting or due-diligence obligations. The entity program should include a trigger to reassess requirements when these events occur.

Date-Stamped Guidance

Because the law changes, internal procedures should identify the date of the legal guidance on which they rely. The compliance team should periodically review agency updates and revise the procedure when necessary.

> ***Practice Note:*** *An entity may be exempt from one federal filing and still be required to provide ownership information to a financial institution, regulator, investor, or transaction counterparty.*

Implementation Checklist

- Verify current federal requirements.
- Identify foreign-formed entities registered in the United States.
- Document exemption or reporting conclusions.
- Protect personal and ownership data.
- Integrate change-event monitoring.
- Review procedures on a scheduled basis.

Key Takeaway

Beneficial-ownership compliance requires current legal verification, accurate ownership records, and careful protection of personal information.

CHAPTER 27.

Entity Health Audits and Remediation

The Purpose of an Entity Audit

An entity health audit tests whether the organization's legal records, public filings, internal data, and operational reality agree. It is especially valuable before financing, acquisition, divestiture, system implementation, or leadership transition.

Audit Scope

A comprehensive audit may review:

- existence and status in domestic and qualified jurisdictions;
- formation documents and amendments;
- current governing documents;
- ownership and capitalization records;
- directors, officers, managers, and authority;
- annual reports, franchise taxes, and licenses;
- registered-agent appointments;
- EIN and tax classification;
- assumed names;
- organizational charts and intercompany agreements;
- transaction approvals;
- minute-book completeness;
- unresolved service of process or legal notices;
- dissolution or withdrawal status of inactive entities.

Risk-Based Prioritization

Not every gap has the same urgency. Prioritize entities involved in active transactions, entities holding material assets, employers, regulated entities, entities with external investors, and entities not in good standing. A missing old receipt may be lower risk than an undocumented ownership transfer.

Remediation Plan

Each finding should identify the issue, affected entity, risk, required action, owner, approver, target date, dependency, and closure evidence.

Remediation may include reinstatement, late filings, tax payments, ratification, amendments, corrected registers, replacement certificates, governing-document updates, or formal dissolution.

Ratification and Correction

Historical gaps often require legal analysis. Do not create backdated documents or assume that a present-day consent can erase the past. Counsel may recommend ratification, validation, correction, or disclosure based on governing law and transaction context.

Reporting

Leadership reports should distinguish critical legal-status issues, material governance gaps, data-quality issues, and administrative cleanup. Progress should be tracked until evidence is complete and the register is reconciled.

> ***Control Point:*** *A remediation item is not closed merely because a document was drafted. Closure requires proper approval, execution or filing, acceptance where applicable, storage, and data update.*

Implementation Checklist

- Define audit scope and risk criteria.
- Compare internal records to official sources.
- Sample high-risk data and documents.
- Create a prioritized remediation tracker.
- Obtain legal review for historical defects.
- Preserve correction and ratification evidence.
- Report progress and recurring root causes.

Key Takeaway

Entity audits convert uncertainty into an actionable risk plan. Remediation should correct both the immediate record and the process that allowed the gap.

PART V

GOVERNANCE ACTIONS AND ORGANIZATIONAL CHANGE

CHAPTER 28.

Governing Body Actions, Minutes, and Written Consents

The Record of Decision

Boards, shareholders, members, managers, partners, and other governing bodies act through procedures established by law and governing documents. Minutes and written consents are not administrative summaries; they are evidence that the entity took action through authorized decision-makers.

Meetings and Written Consents

A meeting typically requires notice, quorum, presentation of matters, voting, and minutes. A written consent permits action without a meeting when authorized and when the required approval threshold is satisfied. The entity manager should confirm which method is available, who must approve, whether unanimous consent is required, and whether notice to nonconsenting persons is necessary.

Preparing the Action

The request should identify the action, business purpose, supporting documents, conflicts, effective date, required approvals, and signatories. Examples include approving contracts, financings, bank authority, acquisitions, dispositions, distributions, officer appointments, tax elections, intercompany arrangements, and changes to governing documents.

Drafting Standards

Resolutions should be precise enough to establish authority without embedding unnecessary operational detail. Defined terms, entity names, transaction documents, dollar amounts, and delegation language should be accurate. Exhibits should be attached or clearly identified. Generic authorization clauses should not be used as a substitute for understanding the action.

Minutes

Minutes should record the date, time, place or method, attendees, notice or waiver, quorum, matters considered, conflicts, decisions, vote results when appropriate, and adjournment. Minutes need not reproduce every discussion, but they should provide a reliable record of process and action.

Execution and Storage

Collect signatures or approvals using an authorized process. Preserve the final consent or approved minutes, signature evidence, exhibits, and related certificates. Update the authority, ownership, and transaction records affected by the action.

> ***Practice Note:*** *Draft the resolutions after reviewing the operative transaction documents. Authority language that does not match the documents can create closing issues.*

Implementation Checklist

- Confirm the correct approving body and threshold.
- Determine meeting or consent requirements.
- Collect complete supporting documents.
- Draft accurate resolutions and exhibits.
- Address conflicts and recusals.
- Preserve final approval evidence.
- Update affected entity data and records.

Key Takeaway

Governance records demonstrate that an entity acted through proper authority. Accuracy of process is as important as the wording of the resolution.

CHAPTER 29.

Officer, Director, Manager, and Member Changes

Why Leadership Changes Require Coordination

Changes in directors, officers, managers, members, partners, trustees, or authorized representatives affect governance, signing authority, banking, licenses, public filings, tax records, insurance, contracts, and access to systems. Human resources may know that a person has departed, but the legal record does not change automatically.

Determine the Legal Mechanism

Review governing documents and law to determine whether the change requires resignation, removal, appointment, election, acceptance, member approval, board approval, or another process. Effective dates matter. A resignation may be effective immediately, on a specified date, or upon acceptance depending on the document and law.

Appointment and Authority

An appointment record should identify the title, person, effective date, term if any, and authority. If the role carries bank, contract, licensing, or regulatory authority, notify the appropriate teams. Limited or transaction-specific authority should be documented separately from general office.

Departures

A departure checklist should address resignations, removal from bank accounts and signature authorities, termination of powers of attorney, return of records, access removal, regulatory notifications, and preservation of prior actions. Do not delete the person's historical role from the register; close it with an end date.

Public and Regulatory Filings

Some jurisdictions require officer, director, manager, or address updates through annual reports or separate filings. Licenses may require immediate notice. The change tracker should identify every affected jurisdiction and system.

Ownership Versus Management

A member or shareholder change is not the same as an officer or manager change. Separate the ownership process from the governance appointment process, even if they occur together.

> ***Control Point:*** *A job title in an internal directory does not establish legal office or authority. Preserve the governing action that created the role.*

Implementation Checklist

- Review governing documents and approval requirements.
- Obtain resignation, removal, or appointment evidence.
- Record effective and end dates.
- Update authority and banking records.
- Review licenses, public filings, and powers of attorney.
- Remove system access while preserving history.
- Notify affected internal and external stakeholders.

Key Takeaway

Leadership changes should flow through a controlled legal process that updates authority, records, systems, and external obligations.

CHAPTER 30.

Amendments and Administrative Changes

Categories of Change

Entities change names, purposes, authorized shares, management structures, registered agents, principal addresses, fiscal years, and other attributes. Some changes require amendments to formation or governing documents. Others require administrative filings, internal approvals, or notices to agencies and counterparties.

Change Intake

The request should state the current information, proposed information, reason, desired effective date, affected jurisdictions, and business impact. Legal and tax should determine which documents and approvals are required.

Name Changes

A legal name change often requires a state amendment, revised foreign qualifications, updated tax records, licenses, bank accounts, insurance, contracts, invoices, websites, assumed names, and internal systems. The project should use a dependency list and communications plan.

Address and Registered-Agent Changes

Address changes can affect tax nexus, licenses, payroll, service of process, and public records. A registered-agent change may require filings in every affected jurisdiction. Confirm the effective date and avoid a gap in coverage.

Purpose and Capital Changes

Changes to purpose, authorized shares, classes, or series may require charter amendments and shareholder or member approval. These are not routine data edits. Coordinate with securities, tax, finance, and transaction counsel as appropriate.

Effective Dates and Evidence

Store the approval, filed amendment, acceptance evidence, amended or restated governing documents, and updated certificates. Preserve prior versions as superseded rather than deleting them.

> ***Practice Note:*** *Create one change map that lists every system, jurisdiction, document, license, bank, insurer, and counterparty affected by the change.*

Implementation Checklist

- Document current and proposed information.
- Identify legal and internal approvals.
- Map affected jurisdictions and systems.
- Prepare and file required amendments.
- Update governing documents and certificates.
- Notify tax, finance, licensing, insurance, banking, and contracts teams.
- Preserve historical versions and effective dates.

Key Takeaway

An amendment is a cross-functional change project. The public filing is only one step in making the organization's records and operations consistent.

CHAPTER 31.

Ownership Changes and Capital Events

Types of Capital Events

Ownership may change through issuance, transfer, redemption, repurchase, contribution, distribution, conversion, exercise, vesting, inheritance, reorganization, or transaction. Each event may affect voting, economics, tax, beneficial ownership, governance rights, and reporting.

Intake and Documentation

The request should identify the parties, entity, interest type, amount or percentage, consideration, effective date, approvals, transfer restrictions, preemptive rights, consents, tax treatment, and conditions. Supporting documents may include purchase agreements, assignments, joinders, subscription agreements, contribution agreements, certificates, powers, and governing-body actions.

Transfer Restrictions

Governing documents may require consent, rights of first refusal, tag-along or drag-along procedures, lender approval, regulatory approval, or admission of the transferee. An executed assignment alone may not complete the change.

Ledger and Schedule Updates

Update the authoritative ownership ledger, schedules to governing documents, cap table, organizational chart, tax and accounting records, and beneficial-ownership analysis. Preserve both pre- and post-transaction ownership with effective dates.

Capital Contributions and Distributions

Finance should confirm receipt or transfer of consideration. Legal approval and financial posting should reconcile. Where a contribution changes ownership or capital accounts, document the effect rather than assuming the accounting entry explains the legal result.

Communication and Confidentiality

Ownership information is sensitive. Limit distribution, use secure channels, and verify the identity and authority of requesters. Fraudulent transfer instructions and impersonation risks should be addressed in the process.

> ***Control Point:*** *Do not update ownership based on a term sheet, draft agreement, or expected closing. Update when the transaction is effective and conditions are satisfied.*

Implementation Checklist

- Review governing-document restrictions.
- Confirm approvals and conditions.
- Verify consideration and effective date.
- Preserve executed transfer and admission documents.
- Update ledgers, schedules, charts, and tax records.
- Reassess beneficial-ownership and licensing obligations.
- Maintain pre- and post-transaction history.

Key Takeaway

Ownership changes require legal, financial, tax, and data reconciliation. The authoritative record should change only when the legal event is complete.

CHAPTER 32.

Intercompany Agreements and Related-Party Governance

Why Intercompany Relationships Need Documentation

Entities within the same group may share employees, services, cash, intellectual property, facilities, insurance, technology, or management. Common ownership does not eliminate the need to document relationships when law, tax, accounting, financing, or governance requires it.

Common Agreements

Intercompany arrangements may include shared-services agreements, management agreements, cost-allocation agreements, intellectual-property licenses, leases, loans, guarantees, cash-pooling arrangements, tax-sharing agreements, employee secondments, and asset-use agreements.

Approval and Conflict Considerations

Related-party transactions may require special approvals under governing documents, conflict policies, lender covenants, or law. The entity manager should identify directors, officers, managers, or owners with interests in the transaction and preserve disclosures, recusals, and approvals.

Entity-Specific Obligations

The agreement should clearly identify the parties, services or assets, pricing or allocation method, term, payment, liability, records, termination, and governing law. Avoid using a parent-company name as shorthand when specific subsidiaries perform or receive the services.

Record and Accounting Reconciliation

Each party's minute book should contain or reference the agreement and approval. Finance should know the effective date and allocation terms. Material amendments and terminations should be documented.

Insolvency and Transaction Readiness

Undocumented intercompany balances can complicate financing, diligence, bankruptcy analysis, and sale. A buyer may require settlement or assignment. An annual review of material intercompany relationships improves readiness.

> ***Practice Note:*** *A shared invoice or accounting allocation is not always a substitute for a legal agreement establishing the rights and obligations of each entity.*

Implementation Checklist

- Inventory material intercompany relationships.
- Confirm legal, tax, and accounting requirements.
- Identify conflicts and approval thresholds.
- Use correct entity parties and effective dates.
- Preserve approvals and executed agreements.
- Reconcile terms with accounting treatment.
- Review arrangements during reorganizations and transactions.

Key Takeaway

Intercompany agreements support separateness, transparency, and transaction readiness by documenting how related entities exchange value and responsibility.

CHAPTER 33.

Mergers, Conversions, and Domestications

Structural Change

Mergers, conversions, and domestications alter the legal form, jurisdiction, or existence of entities. These transactions can affect assets, liabilities, contracts, licenses, tax treatment, employees, financing, ownership, and records. They should be managed as coordinated projects.

Merger

In a merger, one or more entities combine according to a plan and applicable law. The surviving entity may succeed to assets and liabilities by operation of law, subject to exceptions and required consents. The file should include the plan, approvals, certificates, effective time, transaction agreements, and post-merger ownership and governance records.

Conversion

A conversion changes an entity from one legal type to another, such as a corporation to an LLC. The transaction may require a plan, governing-body and owner approval, state filings, new governing documents, ownership conversion terms, tax analysis, and regulatory review.

Domestication

A domestication or continuance changes the entity's jurisdiction while preserving its legal continuity where permitted. Requirements vary. The project may involve filings in both the old and new jurisdictions and updates to foreign qualifications, tax accounts, licenses, contracts, and registered-agent appointments.

Pre-Closing Checklist

Confirm good standing, governing authority, owner approvals, lender and contract consents, tax consequences, employee and benefit implications, licenses, litigation, insurance, banking, and effective time. Prepare a detailed closing and post-closing checklist.

Post-Closing Records

Update the register, organizational chart, ownership, tax classification, entity status, qualifications, licenses, bank accounts, contracts, accounting, and calendars. Preserve predecessor history and do not delete dissolved or converted records.

> ***Control Point:*** *Structural transactions can be legally effective before operational systems are updated. Plan post-closing changes in advance to avoid a period of inconsistent records.*

Implementation Checklist

- Define the transaction structure and effective time.
- Confirm approvals and consents.
- Obtain tax and regulatory review.
- Prepare plans, filings, and new governing documents.
- Coordinate closing evidence.
- Execute a cross-functional post-closing plan.
- Preserve predecessor and successor history.

Key Takeaway

Mergers, conversions, and domestications require lifecycle coordination before and after the filing. The legal event and operational transition must be managed together.

CHAPTER 34.

Special-Purpose Entities and Portfolio Governance

The Purpose of an SPE

A special-purpose entity is formed for a defined asset, project, investment, financing, or transaction. SPEs are common in real estate, renewable energy, structured finance, private equity, securitization, and joint ventures. Their value depends on clear purpose, ownership, restrictions, and separateness.

Standardization With Controlled Exceptions

Portfolio programs benefit from standardized names, formation jurisdictions, governing documents, ownership structures, banking, registered-agent coverage, and compliance calendars. Standardization reduces cycle time and error. Exceptions should be documented and approved because lenders, investors, regulators, or local law may require different terms.

Lifecycle Milestones

An SPE may move through development, acquisition, construction, operation, financing, sale, and dissolution. The register should track lifecycle stage and associated obligations. An entity that appears dormant during development may still hold options, permits, land rights, intellectual property, or contractual obligations.

Financing Requirements

Lenders may require independent managers or directors, separateness covenants, limitations on activities, restricted amendments, special bankruptcy provisions, or specific organizational documents. The entity manager should flag these restrictions so routine governance actions do not violate financing terms.

Scale Controls

Large portfolios need automated naming, intake, template selection, data validation, and dashboard reporting. Batch creation should still preserve entity-specific approvals and evidence. A portfolio audit should identify duplicate entities, inactive entities with recurring costs, missing governing documents, and entities that no longer serve a business purpose.

Exit Planning

The business should decide whether an SPE will be sold with the asset, retained, merged, or dissolved. Contracts, permits, bank accounts, debt, taxes, and records affect the decision.

> ***Practice Note:*** *"Project inactive" does not mean "entity has no obligations." Confirm legal status, assets, contracts, licenses, taxes, and financing before changing the lifecycle designation.*

Implementation Checklist

- Define the SPE's purpose and lifecycle stage.
- Use approved portfolio standards.
- Record financing and governance restrictions.
- Track project-specific assets, contracts, and permits.
- Audit inactive and duplicate entities.
- Plan sale, retention, or dissolution early.

Key Takeaway

SPE portfolios require both standardization and entity-specific discipline. Scale should increase control, not reduce it.

PART VI

TRANSACTIONS, DUE DILIGENCE, AND EXIT

CHAPTER 35.

Entity Due Diligence and Readiness

Readiness Before the Request Arrives

Entity diligence often begins under severe time pressure. A buyer, lender, investor, auditor, or counterparty may request formation documents, amendments, governing documents, ownership, good-standing certificates, qualifications, minutes, consents, licenses, and authority evidence. A mature program maintains these records continuously rather than reconstructing them during a deal.

The Diligence Population

Begin by defining which entities are in scope and why. Reconcile the transaction perimeter to organizational charts, financial schedules, asset lists, and the master register. Hidden subsidiaries and obsolete entities can create delays.

Core Diligence Categories

Typical categories include:

- formation and all amendments;
- governing documents and amendments;
- ownership and capitalization;
- directors, officers, managers, and authority;
- domestic and foreign good standing;
- assumed names, licenses, and permits;
- material governance actions;
- mergers, conversions, and predecessor history;
- liens, litigation, and service-of-process records;
- intercompany agreements and related-party transactions;
- dissolution or inactive status;
- tax identifiers and classifications, subject to access controls.

Quality Control

Documents should be complete, executed, legible, and labeled. Redact sensitive personal information where appropriate and authorized. Compare the data-room population to the register and identify missing or conflicting records before external review.

Exception List

Create a diligence exception list showing the issue, risk, owner, remediation plan, target date, and disclosure approach. Examples include expired good-standing certificates, unsigned governing documents, missing ownership approvals, late annual reports, or unresolved qualifications.

Certifications and Authority

Transactions may require secretary's certificates, incumbency certificates, certified resolutions, or officer certificates. These should be prepared from verified records, not copied from an old transaction without review.

> ***Control Point:*** *A clean data room does not mean every document is present. Use a population checklist and reconcile it to the legal structure.*

Implementation Checklist

- Confirm the transaction entity population.
- Apply a standard diligence checklist.
- Validate document completeness and execution.
- Reconcile ownership, authority, and good standing.
- Create and manage an exception list.
- Prepare current certificates from verified records.
- Preserve the final transaction record.

Key Takeaway

Transaction readiness is the result of continuous entity hygiene. Diligence should validate the record, not create it from scratch.

CHAPTER 36.

UCC, Lien, Judgment, and Litigation Searches

Distinguishing Search Types

An entity status search is not a lien search. A UCC search identifies financing statements filed under Article 9 against a debtor name in specified filing offices. Judgment, tax-lien, litigation, bankruptcy, and local-record searches are separate. The scope should be defined by counsel or the transaction team.

Debtor Name Accuracy

For registered organizations, UCC search and filing rules generally depend on the exact public-organic-record name. Minor name errors can affect results. Confirm the legal name, jurisdiction, entity type, formation record, former names, merger history, and relevant locations before ordering.

Search Scope

A search request should identify:

- entity and exact legal name;
- current and former names;
- formation and operating jurisdictions;
- search types;
- date and time through which results are current;
- federal, state, county, court, bankruptcy, tax, and local sources as applicable;
- copies of underlying filings;
- requested turnaround and certification level.

Reviewing Results

Search reports require legal review. A filing against a similar name may not relate to the entity. A terminated filing may still appear. Continuations, amendments, assignments, and collateral descriptions affect interpretation. The entity manager should organize results and underlying documents without making unsupported legal conclusions.

Payoff and Termination

In a financing or sale, existing liens may require payoff letters, termination statements, releases, or amendments. Track responsible parties, filing conditions, and post-closing evidence. A signed payoff agreement is not the same as a filed termination.

Litigation and Judgment Searches

Court searches may be limited by jurisdiction, indexing, and access. Confirm whether the search covers federal and state courts, party-name variations, and a defined period. Service-of-process records and internal litigation lists should be reconciled.

> ***Practice Note:*** *Always ask what risk the search is intended to address. The right scope for a routine vendor review may be different from the scope for secured financing or acquisition.*

Implementation Checklist

- Confirm exact legal and former names.
- Define jurisdictions and search types.
- Order underlying filing copies.
- Route results for legal interpretation.
- Track payoff, release, and termination requirements.
- Preserve final searches and post-closing evidence.

Key Takeaway

Lien and litigation searches are scoped investigations. Accuracy of names, jurisdictions, and review matters more than a generic "clear" label.

CHAPTER 37.

Financing and Transaction Closings

Entity Management at Closing

Entity records support representations, conditions precedent, signature authority, legal opinions, certificates, and lender diligence. A missing consent or status issue can delay funding even when the commercial terms are complete.

Closing Checklist

The entity workstream may include:

- domestic and foreign good-standing certificates;
- certified formation documents;
- governing documents and amendments;
- incumbency and secretary's certificates;
- board, member, manager, or shareholder approvals;
- officer appointments and signature authority;
- ownership charts;
- UCC searches and filing authorizations;
- payoff, release, and lien-termination documents;
- bring-down certificates;
- legal-opinion support;
- post-closing filing and record tasks.

Signature Management

Confirm the exact entity party and authorized signer for each document. Signature packets should use approved titles and blocks. Escrowed signatures should be handled according to counsel's instructions. The final record should show what was executed and released at closing.

Certificate Preparation

Certificates should be based on current records and dated appropriately. Attachments must match the certified documents. A secretary or authorized officer should understand the certification and sign under proper authority.

Closing Evidence

After closing, collect final executed agreements, certificates, filed UCC records, state filings, funds evidence as appropriate, and a closing set or index. Update the entity register for new debt, ownership, restrictions, officers, or status.

Post-Closing Obligations

Track delayed filings, original documents, post-closing consents, lien terminations, good-standing deliveries, bank changes, and covenant calendars. Closing is not complete when funds move if the entity workstream remains open.

> ***Control Point:*** *Verify every certificate attachment and signature title against current governing records on the date of closing.*

Implementation Checklist

- Maintain an entity-specific closing checklist.
- Verify parties, signers, and approvals.
- Order certificates with sufficient lead time.
- Prepare accurate incumbency and authority evidence.
- Preserve final closing documents and filings.
- Update entity data and covenant calendars.
- Close post-closing items with evidence.

Key Takeaway

Entity management provides the proof of existence, authority, and compliance that allows transactions to close.

CHAPTER 38.

Acquisitions, Divestitures, and Post-Closing Integration

Acquiring a New Entity Population

An acquisition transfers not only assets and obligations but also entity records, deadlines, vendors, licenses, accounts, and historical risk. The integration team should obtain a complete entity inventory and define which systems and teams will own the records after closing.

Day-One Priorities

Immediate priorities include service-of-process routing, bank and signer authority, critical licenses, insurance, tax deadlines, payroll, registered agents, access to records, and transaction-required officer or director changes. Some changes must occur at closing; others can follow under a controlled plan.

Data Migration

Map acquired data to the organization's data dictionary. Preserve original source records and distinguish verified data from unverified imports. Duplicate names, inconsistent jurisdiction codes, missing ownership dates, and stale officer records are common.

Governance Integration

Review governing documents, reserved powers, investor rights, debt restrictions, and joint-venture approvals before applying standard templates. Acquired entities may have obligations that prevent immediate standardization.

Divestitures

For a sale, define which entities, records, contracts, licenses, bank accounts, and employees transfer. The seller may need copies of records for tax, litigation, or retention. Access should be separated at closing, and service of process should route correctly after the change.

Transitional Services

If the seller continues to provide entity management, tax, accounting, or registered-agent support, document the services, duration, fees, data access, and exit steps. Transitional arrangements should not leave authority ambiguous.

> ***Practice Note:*** *Do not overwrite acquired history to make the portfolio look uniform. Preserve history, then standardize prospectively with documented changes.*

Implementation Checklist

- Obtain a complete entity and obligation inventory.
- Prioritize day-one legal-status and notice controls.
- Migrate data with validation and source references.
- Review legacy governance and financing restrictions.
- Separate divested records and access.
- Document transitional services and exit milestones.
- Complete a post-closing entity audit.

Key Takeaway

Acquisition and divestiture integration is a controlled transfer of legal identity, records, authority, and obligations.

CHAPTER 39.

Dissolution, Withdrawal, and Wind-Down

Choosing the Correct Exit

An entity may be sold, merged out of existence, converted, domesticated, withdrawn from a foreign jurisdiction, administratively dissolved, or voluntarily dissolved. These outcomes are different. The business and counsel should identify the intended legal result and confirm that the entity no longer needs to hold assets, contracts, licenses, claims, or obligations.

Approval and Planning

Review governing documents, financing agreements, investor rights, contracts, and law for approval requirements. The wind-down plan should identify assets, liabilities, employees, taxes, bank accounts, insurance, licenses, litigation, contracts, intellectual property, records, and stakeholder communications.

Foreign Withdrawals

Before domestic dissolution, identify every state where the entity is qualified. Withdrawal may require final reports, tax clearance, agent consent, or a designated address for future service. Failing to withdraw can allow annual obligations to continue.

State Dissolution Filing

The filing may be called articles or a certificate of dissolution, cancellation, termination, or similar name. Confirm required approvals, effective date, tax prerequisites, and whether claims-notice procedures are appropriate.

Administrative Dissolution

Allowing an entity to lapse for nonpayment is not a controlled wind-down. Administrative dissolution may leave liabilities, tax obligations, and reinstatement issues. Voluntary closure generally provides better evidence and coordination.

Status Tracking

Use lifecycle statuses such as wind-down approved, operations ceased, liabilities pending, withdrawals pending, domestic filing submitted, dissolved, and records archived. Do not mark the entity closed while material obligations remain.

> ***Control Point:*** *Obtain written confirmation from tax, finance, treasury, legal, and the business owner before final dissolution when their obligations are relevant.*

Implementation Checklist

- Confirm the correct exit structure.
- Obtain governing approvals.
- Inventory assets, liabilities, contracts, and jurisdictions.
- Complete foreign withdrawals and tax clearances.
- File domestic dissolution documents.
- Preserve acceptance evidence and update status.
- Continue tracking surviving obligations.

Key Takeaway

Dissolution is the final stage of a coordinated wind-down, not the first step and not a substitute for closing the business.

CHAPTER 40.

Tax, Contract, Employee, and Asset Closure

Cross-Functional Closure

The legal entity may remain necessary until tax returns, contracts, claims, assets, employees, and accounts are addressed. The wind-down manager should maintain one integrated checklist with named owners and evidence.

Tax and Accounting

Tax may need final federal, state, local, payroll, sales, property, and franchise filings. Accounting should close books, reconcile balances, settle intercompany accounts, and preserve financial records. The entity should not be dissolved on an assumed date that conflicts with tax treatment.

Contracts

Identify contracts to terminate, assign, novate, expire, or retain. Review notice periods, consent requirements, survival clauses, indemnities, warranties, confidentiality, and records obligations. Preserve termination and assignment evidence.

Employees and Benefits

Human resources and employment counsel should address notice, final pay, benefits, records, immigration, WARN or similar obligations, and transfer to affiliates or buyers. Entity closure does not eliminate employment obligations.

Assets and Intellectual Property

Transfer or dispose of real estate, equipment, cash, accounts, intellectual property, data, permits, claims, and records. Document consideration and approvals. Confirm that assets have not been left in a dissolved entity.

Bank Accounts, Insurance, and Licenses

Close bank accounts only after outstanding checks, refunds, taxes, and claims are addressed. Review tail coverage, occurrence coverage, claims reporting, bond cancellation, permit surrender, and license transfer. Keep a receiving address and contact for post-closure correspondence.

> ***Practice Note:*** *A "zero balance" in accounting does not prove that the entity has no legal obligations. Contracts, claims, taxes, and records may survive.*

Implementation Checklist

- Obtain tax and accounting closure confirmation.
- Terminate or transfer contracts.
- Address employee and benefit obligations.
- Transfer or dispose of all assets.
- Close licenses, permits, bank accounts, and insurance.
- Settle intercompany balances.
- Preserve evidence of each closure action.

Key Takeaway

A lawful and orderly wind-down requires coordinated closure of every function that used the entity.

CHAPTER 41.

Preservation of Records and Survival Obligations

The Entity Ends; Obligations May Continue

Dissolution does not erase history. Tax audits, litigation, indemnities, warranties, environmental obligations, employee claims, data obligations, contract survival clauses, and record-retention requirements may continue. The organization must identify who will maintain records and respond after the entity ceases to exist.

Final Minute Book

The final record should include approvals, wind-down plan, creditor or claimant notices if used, tax clearances, withdrawals, dissolution filing, acceptance evidence, asset distributions, contract terminations, license closures, bank closure, insurance information, and final ownership or distribution records.

Custodian and Access

Assign a records custodian and successor contact. Preserve access rights for legal, tax, finance, and litigation teams. If the entity is sold, the purchase agreement should address which party retains originals, receives copies, and controls access.

Service and Claims

Some jurisdictions require a post-dissolution address or agent for claims. Registered-agent services may need to continue for a period. Maintain a process for mail and legal notices after closure.

Retention Periods

Apply the organization's approved retention schedule, with legal and tax review. Permanent governance records should remain identifiable. Sensitive data should remain protected throughout retention and secure destruction.

Lessons Learned

After a major wind-down, review the process. Identify recurring obstacles such as unknown bank accounts, missing contracts, stale qualifications, unclear ownership, or unassigned licenses. Feed the lessons into onboarding and ongoing controls.

> ***Control Point:*** *Do not archive the entity until all open items, custodians, survival obligations, and access arrangements are documented.*

Implementation Checklist

- Assemble the final entity record.
- Assign a records custodian and successor contact.
- Preserve post-dissolution service arrangements.
- Apply legal holds and retention schedules.
- Document surviving contracts and claims.
- Restrict and monitor access to sensitive records.
- Conduct a post-mortem and improve the program.

Key Takeaway

The final responsibility of entity management is to preserve the evidence and access needed after the legal entity's active life ends.

PART VII

LEGAL OPERATIONS, TECHNOLOGY, AND PROGRAM SCALE

CHAPTER 42.

Vendor and Registered-Agent Management

The Vendor Portfolio

Entity management may rely on registered-agent providers, filing services, entity management platforms, document custodians, search vendors, translation and authentication services, and outside counsel. Vendors extend the legal team's capacity, but responsibility for accuracy and compliance remains with the organization.

Selection Criteria

Evaluate geographic coverage, service quality, security, integration capability, reporting, escalation, turnaround, pricing, account management, data ownership, export rights, business continuity, and termination support. A low per-entity fee may be offset by document charges, filing markups, rush fees, or poor invoice transparency.

Service-Level Expectations

Service levels should address notice transmission, order confirmation, rejection handling, portal availability, data export, billing detail, and response time. Service of process and transaction-critical filings require heightened standards.

Invoice and Coverage Reconciliation

At least periodically, compare the vendor's entity list to the master register and official state records. Identify duplicate services, entities sold or dissolved, missing jurisdictions, and unauthorized orders. Require invoice detail by entity, jurisdiction, service period, government fee, service fee, and rush fee.

Data and Exit Rights

Contracts should address confidentiality, security, incident notification, subcontractors, data location, audit rights, record retention, ownership of uploaded documents, and export upon termination. The organization should be able to leave without losing its records or history.

Performance Reviews

Use a scorecard that measures accuracy, timeliness, escalation, invoice quality, service recovery, security, reporting, and account support. Document chronic failures and corrective actions.

> ***Practice Note:*** *A vendor's portal should reconcile to the organization's system of record. It should not silently become a second, conflicting master database.*

Implementation Checklist

- Define required services and coverage.
- Conduct legal, security, and financial diligence.
- Negotiate service levels and data rights.
- Reconcile vendor coverage and invoices.
- Track performance and remediation.
- Maintain a transition and export plan.

Key Takeaway

Vendor management is a control function. Strong contracts, reconciliation, and performance monitoring protect the entity portfolio.

CHAPTER 43.

Budget, Invoices, and Cost Controls

Understanding the Cost Base

Entity costs include formation fees, annual reports, franchise taxes, registered-agent services, licenses, certificates, searches, apostilles, rush fees, outside counsel, and technology. Without structured coding, the legal team cannot distinguish unavoidable government costs from controllable service costs.

Budget Design

Build the budget from the entity inventory and obligation calendar. Separate recurring costs from transaction-driven and remediation costs. Account for new formations, expected qualifications, acquisitions, divestitures, rate increases, and contingency.

Invoice Review

Each charge should identify the entity, jurisdiction, service, government fee, vendor fee, date, and requestor. Compare the invoice to the approved order and evidence of completion. Investigate duplicate charges, services for inactive entities, unsupported rush fees, and markups.

Credit Card and Expense Reconciliation

If filings are paid by card, maintain an order log with receipt, entity, matter or cost center, filing type, amount, government fee, service fee, and accounting code. Reconcile the statement to the order log and repository. Missing receipts should be resolved promptly.

Accruals and Forecasts

Coordinate with finance on accrual timing and material taxes or transaction costs. Forecast by month or quarter based on due dates. Variance reports should explain new entities, penalties, rush activity, tax changes, and vendor-rate changes.

Cost Reduction

Savings can come from eliminating duplicate coverage, dissolving unused entities, consolidating vendors, negotiating volume pricing, reducing rush orders, using direct filings where appropriate, and improving invoice audits. Cost reduction should not weaken service-of-process or compliance controls.

> ***Control Point:*** *Government fees, taxes, vendor fees, and penalties should be reported separately. Combining them hides avoidable cost.*

Implementation Checklist

- Build the budget from entity and obligation data.
- Use entity-level invoice coding.
- Reconcile charges to approved orders and evidence.
- Separate government, service, rush, and penalty costs.
- Forecast recurring and transaction costs.
- Audit duplicate and inactive-entity charges.
- Report savings and avoided penalties.

Key Takeaway

A disciplined cost model allows legal operations to control spend without compromising compliance or response quality.

CHAPTER 44.

Metrics, Dashboards, and Reporting

Metrics With a Purpose

Metrics should help leaders understand risk, workload, cost, speed, quality, and capacity. Counting the number of entities is useful, but it does not reveal whether the portfolio is healthy. Choose measures that support decisions and improvement.

Core Metrics

A balanced dashboard may include:

- active, inactive, wind-down, and dissolved entities;
- formations, qualifications, withdrawals, and dissolutions by period;
- obligations due in thirty, sixty, and ninety days;
- on-time filing rate;
- rejected or late filing rate;
- entities not in good standing;
- missing governing or ownership records;
- service-of-process routing time;
- formation and certificate cycle time;
- open remediation items by severity;
- vendor accuracy and response time;
- budget versus actual and penalties avoided;
- data-completeness and reconciliation scores.

Definitions and Context

Every metric needs a definition, data source, calculation, owner, frequency, and target. "Cycle time" may begin at request submission, approval, or vendor order. Without a standard, comparisons are misleading.

Executive Reporting

Leaders usually need trends and exceptions rather than operational detail. Present material status issues, upcoming transaction risks, overdue obligations, root causes, cost variance, and decisions needed. Use clear categories such as red, amber, and green only when criteria are defined.

Operational Reporting

The working team needs task-level reports, aging, workload by owner, rejection reasons, and missing data. Dashboards should allow drill-down without exposing restricted information to unauthorized users.

Avoiding Vanity Metrics

A high number of completed filings may reflect portfolio size, not performance. Pair volume with quality and timeliness. Report the number of entities remediated and the reduction in risk, not only the number of documents uploaded.

> ***Practice Note:*** *A useful metric leads to a question, decision, or action. If no one changes behavior based on it, reconsider whether it belongs on the dashboard.*

Implementation Checklist

- Select risk, quality, time, cost, and capacity measures.
- Define calculations and data owners.
- Separate executive and operational views.
- Set targets and escalation thresholds.
- Validate data before publication.
- Review trends and root causes.
- Retire metrics that do not support action.

Key Takeaway

Metrics turn entity management from invisible administrative work into a measurable legal operations program.

CHAPTER 45.

Technology Selection and Implementation

Start With the Operating Model

Technology should support a defined process, not substitute for one. Before selecting a platform, document the entity lifecycle, roles, data dictionary, records taxonomy, approvals, reports, security needs, integrations, and pain points. A platform configured around an unclear process will automate confusion.

Requirements

Requirements may include entity and ownership records, effective-dated history, compliance calendars, document storage, workflow, e-signature, organizational charts, reporting, API access, bulk import, role-based security, audit logs, service-of-process integration, vendor feeds, and data export.

Evaluation

Use realistic demonstrations based on the organization's scenarios. Ask vendors to show a formation request, ownership change, foreign qualification, annual filing, service-of-process notice, transaction report, and system exit. Evaluate usability for both administrators and occasional business users.

Data Migration

Profile and clean source data before migration. Map fields, controlled values, ownership relationships, document categories, and historical records. Test a representative sample, reconcile counts and key fields, and preserve the legacy source until acceptance.

Configuration Governance

Assign owners for fields, workflows, permissions, templates, and reports. Avoid excessive customization that makes upgrades difficult. Document configuration decisions and maintain a change process.

Adoption

Train users by role and scenario. Provide intake instructions, data standards, and quick reference materials. Measure adoption through request volume, completion rates, search success, and reduction in off-system work.

Exit Planning

Before implementation, confirm that data, documents, metadata, and audit history can be exported in usable formats. Include termination assistance in the contract.

> ***Control Point:*** *Do not migrate inaccurate ownership or status data merely to meet a launch date. Mark unverified data and remediate it visibly.*

Implementation Checklist

- Document processes and requirements first.
- Evaluate realistic end-to-end scenarios.
- Conduct security and privacy review.
- Clean and map source data.
- Test migration and reconcile results.
- Establish configuration governance.
- Train users and measure adoption.
- Preserve export and exit rights.

Key Takeaway

Technology succeeds when it reinforces a clear operating model, trusted data, and accountable ownership.

CHAPTER 46.

Workflow Automation and Responsible AI

Appropriate Automation

Automation can route requests, validate fields, generate standard documents, calculate deadlines, send reminders, create folders, update statuses, reconcile invoices, and produce dashboards. It is most effective for repeatable, rules-based work with clear inputs and exceptions.

Designing the Workflow

Map the current process before automating. Identify trigger, required data, decision points, approvals, system updates, evidence, exceptions, and closure. Remove unnecessary steps before building automation.

Document Generation

Templates can generate formation documents, consents, certificates, checklists, and reports from approved data. Use controlled clauses, jurisdiction logic, version control, and legal review. Generated documents should be reviewed before execution or filing.

Responsible Use of AI

Generative AI can assist with summarizing records, classifying documents, drafting routine communications, identifying inconsistencies, and creating first drafts. It should not make unsupervised legal conclusions, determine authority, or file documents without review. Confidentiality, privilege, data use, hallucination, bias, and retention must be addressed.

Human Review

Define which outputs require legal review, tax review, second-person verification, or approval. High-risk fields such as ownership, tax identifiers, effective dates, and signer authority should not be changed solely by automated inference.

Monitoring

Automations can fail silently when a field changes, an integration breaks, or a rule becomes outdated. Monitor exceptions, rejected filings, duplicate tasks, missed triggers, and user overrides. Assign an owner for each automation.

> ***Practice Note:*** *Automate the evidence trail as well as the task. A workflow that files a report but fails to preserve acceptance evidence is incomplete.*

Implementation Checklist

- Select stable, rules-based processes.
- Map and simplify before automation.
- Use controlled templates and data sources.
- Define human-review thresholds.
- Protect confidential and personal information.
- Test exceptions and failure modes.
- Monitor performance and legal changes.

Key Takeaway

Automation and AI can increase speed and consistency, but accountability, review, and evidence must remain explicit.

CHAPTER 47.

Standard Operating Procedures, Training, and Knowledge Transfer

The Purpose of an SOP

A standard operating procedure explains how a process should be performed, by whom, using which controls, and with what evidence. It should make work repeatable without turning judgment into a script.

SOP Structure

A strong SOP includes purpose, scope, definitions, roles, prerequisites, step-by-step procedure, decision points, approvals, service levels, evidence requirements, exceptions, escalation, records, metrics, and revision history. Screenshots may be useful for a current system, but they should not replace process logic and should be updated when interfaces change.

Vendor-Neutral Design

Core procedures should use functional terms such as "entity management system," "registered-agent portal," and "document repository." System-specific work instructions can be maintained separately. This prevents the entire policy from becoming obsolete when a vendor changes.

Training by Role

Entity administrators need detailed process training. Business requestors need concise intake and approval guidance. Executives need decision rights and risk. Finance and tax need handoffs and calendars. Training should use realistic scenarios and include how to escalate uncertainty.

Knowledge Transfer

Transitions should include portfolio overview, upcoming deadlines, open transactions, unresolved remediation, vendor contacts, system access, reporting cadence, sensitive data procedures, and key historical decisions. A checklist and shadow period reduce dependence on memory.

Document Governance

Each SOP should have an owner, approval date, effective date, review date, version, and change log. Retire superseded copies and notify affected users of material changes.

> ***Control Point:*** *A procedure should state what proves completion. Without evidence, two people may perform the same task differently and both believe it is closed.*

Implementation Checklist

- Use a standard SOP template.
- Separate policy from system-specific instructions.
- Define controls, exceptions, and evidence.
- Train users by role and scenario.
- Maintain revision history and review dates.
- Use formal knowledge-transfer checklists.
- Test procedures through periodic walkthroughs.

Key Takeaway

SOPs preserve institutional knowledge and convert individual expertise into a resilient organizational capability.

CHAPTER 48.

Scaling Entity Management Programs

Scale Changes the Control Model

A program managing ten entities can rely on direct knowledge and manual review. A program managing hundreds requires standardized data, role specialization, automation, exception reporting, portfolio segmentation, and capacity planning.

Segmentation

Segment entities by risk, activity, jurisdiction, ownership, transaction status, regulation, and lifecycle stage. High-risk entities may require quarterly reviews; dormant domestic subsidiaries may require annual review. Segmentation allows resources to follow risk.

Service Model

Define which tasks are centralized, delegated, outsourced, or self-service. Centralize ownership data, governance records, service of process, and critical compliance. Business teams may provide operational facts, but the legal team should control the official record.

Capacity Planning

Measure request volume, recurring obligations, transaction peaks, average cycle time, exception rate, and time per process. Include vendor management, audit, reporting, training, and remediation—not only filings. Build backup coverage for critical deadlines.

Portfolio Rationalization

Periodic reviews should identify entities with no assets, contracts, employees, licenses, tax purpose, or strategic value. Rationalization can reduce fees and complexity, but dissolution requires cross-functional approval and proper wind-down.

Governance Forums

Large programs benefit from a periodic entity governance committee or working group involving legal, tax, finance, treasury, accounting, compliance, and business representatives. The forum can approve standards, resolve ownership questions, prioritize remediation, and review portfolio changes.

Maturity Stages

Programs often move from reactive tracking, to standardized process, to integrated technology, to predictive risk and portfolio optimization. Improvement should be measured against business need rather than technology alone.

> ***Practice Note:*** *Scale problems often appear first as data conflicts and rush requests. Treat them as signals that intake, ownership, or planning needs redesign.*

Implementation Checklist

- Segment the portfolio by risk and lifecycle.
- Define centralized and distributed responsibilities.
- Measure capacity and seasonal demand.
- Build backup coverage and escalation.
- Conduct portfolio rationalization.
- Establish cross-functional governance.
- Maintain a multi-year maturity roadmap.

Key Takeaway

Scaling requires intentional design. Standardization, segmentation, and exception management allow control to grow with the portfolio.

CHAPTER 49.

Remediation, Crisis Response, and Continuous Improvement

When the Program Is Tested

Entity programs are tested by missed filings, loss of good standing, rejected transactions, fraudulent instructions, service-of-process failures, data breaches, tax notices, ownership disputes, and discovered historical defects. The response should stabilize the immediate risk while preserving evidence and addressing root cause.

Triage

Determine the affected entities, jurisdictions, deadlines, legal consequences, transactions, assets, and stakeholders. Assign an incident lead and create a facts log. Avoid speculation and preserve relevant records.

Immediate Controls

Actions may include reinstatement, emergency filings, notice to insurers, litigation response, bank holds, access suspension, correction of public records, preservation notices, or leadership escalation. Counsel should direct legal conclusions and external communications.

Root-Cause Analysis

After stabilization, ask why the failure occurred. Common causes include unclear ownership, stale data, unmonitored inboxes, vendor errors, missing backup, manual reentry, inadequate review, or an outdated SOP. Correct the system, not only the record.

Corrective Action

A corrective-action plan should identify the issue, risk, action, owner, deadline, evidence, validation, and preventive control. Material issues may require leadership or audit reporting.

Continuous Improvement

Use rejection reasons, late tasks, duplicate charges, audit findings, and user feedback to improve forms, training, automation, vendor service levels, and dashboards. Schedule process reviews rather than waiting for crisis.

> ***Control Point:*** *Do not conceal or silently correct material errors. Preserve the original record, document the correction, and escalate according to policy.*

Implementation Checklist

- Establish an incident and remediation protocol.
- Triage legal, operational, and transaction impact.
- Preserve facts and evidence.
- Implement immediate risk controls.
- Perform root-cause analysis.
- Track corrective and preventive actions.
- Report lessons and update procedures.

Key Takeaway

A mature program responds transparently, corrects the record, and improves the control that failed.

PART VIII

APPLIED CASE STUDIES

CHAPTER 50.

Case Study: High-Growth Technology Company

Scenario

A venture-backed software company expands from one corporation to a group containing a parent, an intellectual-property subsidiary, international affiliates, and local employing entities. Formation requests arrive through email, equity records are maintained by finance, annual filings are handled by outside counsel, and no one owns the complete entity list.

Risks

The company faces inconsistent ownership records, untracked foreign qualifications, contracts signed by the wrong entity, duplicate registered-agent services, and missing board approvals for intercompany intellectual-property arrangements. A financing round exposes the gaps.

Program Design

The legal operations team creates a master register with ownership, directors, officers, qualifications, tax classification, and document links. It centralizes formation intake and requires tax, finance, and legal approval. The team builds digital minute books, reconciles the cap table to legal issuances, and establishes quarterly governance reviews.

A contract intake field requires selection of the contracting entity and provides approved signature blocks. Intercompany agreements are inventoried and approved. Annual filings move to a centralized calendar with independent verification.

Outcome

The next financing diligence process produces complete records within days rather than weeks. The company also identifies two unnecessary qualifications and one dormant subsidiary for controlled dissolution.

Lessons

Rapid growth does not excuse weak records. The earlier the company defines ownership of entity data and governance actions, the easier it is to scale investment, international expansion, and transaction readiness.

CHAPTER 51.

Case Study: Renewable Energy Project Portfolio

Scenario

A developer manages a large portfolio of project companies formed to hold site rights, permits, interconnection agreements, equipment contracts, financing, and operating assets. Projects frequently change names, stages, owners, and transaction status.

Risks

A project may be inactive operationally but still hold a lease option or permit. A financing may require a clean chain of ownership, current good standing, lender-approved governing documents, and separateness covenants. Generic folder names and inconsistent project codes make records difficult to locate.

Program Design

The legal team links each project company to a project identifier, lifecycle stage, asset location, ownership, domestic jurisdiction, qualification states, land rights, permits, financing restrictions, and transaction status. Formation uses approved templates with documented exceptions.

A project-gate process requires legal confirmation before development, financing, sale, or abandonment. The transaction checklist includes title, contract, permit, lien, governance, and entity-status workstreams. Inactive projects undergo a quarterly review to determine retention, sale, assignment, or dissolution.

Outcome

The organization reduces rush formations, improves closing readiness, and avoids dissolving entities that still hold valuable rights. Portfolio reporting allows leadership to see legal costs and risks by project stage.

Lessons

Project companies should be managed as both legal entities and components of an asset lifecycle. Data must connect entity status to the underlying project.

CHAPTER 52.

Case Study: Private Equity Acquisition Platform

Scenario

A private equity sponsor acquires companies through holding and acquisition subsidiaries. Each transaction creates entities quickly, and post-closing integration varies by deal team.

Risks

The sponsor lacks a complete view of portfolio ownership, joint-venture rights, management appointments, debt restrictions, and registered-agent coverage. Acquired entities remain on legacy vendor accounts, and transaction folders do not consistently feed the official records.

Program Design

A transaction-onboarding standard requires an entity population, ownership chart, governance matrix, debt restrictions, good-standing evidence, licenses, and record-transfer plan. Day-one changes and post-closing tasks are separated. Data is migrated with verification status.

The sponsor establishes a portfolio entity governance forum and standardized reporting from operating companies. Vendor contracts require entity-level billing and data export. Quarterly reports identify status issues, upcoming maturities, open remediation, and entities eligible for rationalization.

Outcome

The sponsor gains a consistent portfolio view without eliminating necessary local governance. Divestitures become faster because transaction history and ownership records are available.

Lessons

Acquisition platforms need a repeatable bridge from deal execution to permanent entity governance. The closing binder is not a substitute for operational integration.

CHAPTER 53.

Case Study: Multistate Operating Company

Scenario

A services company hires employees and signs customer contracts across many states. Business teams assume that payroll registration or a customer contract automatically determines foreign-qualification requirements.

Risks

The company has inconsistent registrations, annual reports in states where operations ended, missing business licenses, and uncoordinated tax and legal calendars. Some entities are in good standing with the filing office but delinquent for tax purposes.

Program Design

Legal, tax, payroll, human resources, and licensing create a shared state-entry questionnaire. Counsel determines qualification based on facts. Each approved state entry triggers legal registration, tax and payroll setup, licenses, registered-agent coverage, and calendar tasks.

A state-exit checklist requires employee, contract, tax, license, and legal confirmation before withdrawal. The dashboard distinguishes Secretary of State status from tax status.

Outcome

The company reduces duplicate registrations, closes obsolete states, and identifies obligations earlier when new employees are hired.

Lessons

Multistate compliance is cross-functional. No single event—hiring, contracting, banking, or revenue—should be treated as a universal legal conclusion.

CHAPTER 54.

Case Study: Real Estate Ownership Structure

Scenario

A real estate group uses separate LLCs for properties and holding companies for investment interests. Property managers, lenders, and local counsel maintain different records.

Risks

Leases and vendor contracts use trade names, bank accounts are opened with outdated authority, local licenses are not connected to the correct owner, and property sales reveal missing member consents and assignments.

Program Design

The entity register links each LLC to the property address, parcel, lender, manager, ownership, insurance, bank account, licenses, and major contracts. Approved signature blocks distinguish the property owner from the property manager.

Acquisition and disposition checklists require governing approvals, good standing, title-entity confirmation, lien searches, contract assignments, bank and insurance updates, and post-closing record assembly. Annual reviews reconcile property records to entity ownership.

Outcome

The group reduces wrong-party contracts and can prepare sale diligence efficiently. Dormant entities are retained or dissolved based on documented tax and liability analysis.

Lessons

Real estate entity management must connect legal ownership to physical assets, local operations, and financing.

CHAPTER 55.

Case Study: Nonprofit and Mission-Driven Organization

Scenario

A nonprofit organization operates through a parent charity, affiliated foundations, and local entities. Board members rotate frequently, and program staff focus on mission delivery rather than governance records.

Risks

State charitable registrations, annual corporate reports, tax filings, conflict disclosures, and board terms are tracked separately. Restricted gifts and related-party arrangements lack consistent approval records.

Program Design

The organization creates a governance calendar combining board meetings, officer elections, corporate filings, charitable registrations, tax returns, policy reviews, and conflict questionnaires. The register tracks directors, terms, committees, officers, tax-exempt status, and state registrations.

Meeting materials use standardized agendas and resolution templates. Related-party transactions receive conflict review and documented recusals. The minute book separates public filings from confidential board materials.

Outcome

Board transitions become orderly, state registrations remain current, and auditors can trace governance approvals.

Lessons

Mission does not reduce the need for legal operations. Strong governance protects charitable assets, public trust, and continuity.

PART IX

ADVANCED ENTITY GOVERNANCE AND ASSURANCE

CHAPTER 56.

Power of Attorney and Delegation Management

Authority Beyond Formal Office

Organizations frequently authorize employees, agents, counsel, tax professionals, customs brokers, project managers, or other representatives to act through a power of attorney or delegation. These instruments can enable efficient operations, but they also create risk if the scope, duration, revocation, and recordkeeping are unclear.

Types of Authority

A power of attorney may be general or limited, durable or transaction-specific, and governed by statute, contract, or agency requirements. A delegation may arise under bylaws, an operating agreement, a board resolution, an officer's authority, or an internal policy. The entity manager should distinguish between an internal approval to act and an external legal instrument that a bank, agency, or counterparty will rely on.

Required Data

The authority register should identify the granting entity, authorized person, scope, effective date, expiration date, governing approval, permitted subdelegation, geographic or transaction limits, and revocation status. Store the executed instrument and any acceptance, certification, or specimen signature required by the recipient.

Review and Approval

Before issuing authority, confirm that the grantor has power to delegate, the scope is necessary, and the duration is appropriate. High-risk powers involving banking, real estate, borrowing, tax filings, litigation, government submissions, or asset transfers should receive legal review and heightened approval.

Monitoring and Revocation

Use expiration dates whenever practical. Review open powers at least annually and upon role changes, termination, transaction completion, entity sale, or dissolution. Revocation should be documented and communicated to every person or institution that may rely on the authority. Removing internal system access does not revoke an external power of attorney.

Fraud and Misuse Controls

Verify requests independently, especially when authority affects money or ownership. Avoid open-ended authority based on an email. Use dual review, transaction limits, and notice requirements. Preserve a record of documents executed under the authority where feasible.

> ***Control Point:*** *A power of attorney should never remain active merely because no one remembers why it was issued.*

Implementation Checklist

- Inventory powers of attorney and delegations.
- Record scope, dates, grantor, and grantee.
- Confirm the legal basis for delegation.
- Use limited authority and expiration where possible.
- Review upon personnel and transaction changes.
- Document revocation and external notice.
- Retain evidence of actions taken under authority.

Key Takeaway

Delegated authority should be treated as a controlled legal asset. Clear scope, monitoring, and revocation protect both the entity and the authorized representative.

CHAPTER 57.

Contracting Entity Controls

Why the Contracting Entity Matters

The legal entity named in a contract determines who receives rights, bears obligations, owns work product, provides indemnities, recognizes revenue, and may be sued. Business teams often use brand names, parent names, or familiar abbreviations without confirming which entity should sign.

Contract-Party Decision Framework

The selection should consider which entity owns the relevant asset, employs the personnel, holds the license, provides the service, receives payment, carries insurance, bears tax obligations, and has authority under financing or governance documents. The correct answer may differ among customer, vendor, lease, employment, financing, or intellectual-property agreements.

Intake Controls

Contract intake should require the requestor to identify the proposed entity and business rationale. The system should provide verified legal names, jurisdictions, notice addresses, and signature blocks. Requests involving a new entity, affiliate guarantee, shared services, or asset transfer should route for legal and finance review.

Signature Blocks and Authority

A signature block should use the exact legal name and the signer's authorized title or capacity. If a manager, member, general partner, trustee, or attorney-in-fact signs, the capacity should be clear. Trade names may be referenced, but the legal party should not be ambiguous.

Contract Repository Reconciliation

The contract record should include the entity party as structured data. Periodic reports can identify contracts assigned to nonexistent, dissolved, or incorrect entities. During reorganizations, name changes, mergers, and divestitures, contract-party data should drive consent and assignment analysis.

Guarantees and Affiliate Support

A parent or affiliate guarantee is a separate legal commitment and should not be implied by brand use or common ownership. Obtain required approvals and record contingent obligations.

> ***Practice Note:*** *Publish an approved entity directory for contract users, but require legal review when the choice is not obvious. A directory is a control aid, not a substitute for analysis.*

Implementation Checklist

- Require entity selection in contract intake.
- Maintain verified names, addresses, and signature blocks.
- Confirm asset, employee, license, tax, and revenue alignment.
- Document guarantees and affiliate obligations separately.
- Capture entity parties as contract metadata.
- Reconcile contracts during structural changes.
- Escalate unclear or mixed-party arrangements.

Key Takeaway

Contracting entity controls connect the legal structure to day-to-day business. They prevent obligations from landing in the wrong company.

CHAPTER 58.

Tax and Legal Entity Reconciliation

Two Records of the Same Organization

Legal and tax teams may maintain different but related views of an entity. Legal tracks state-law existence, ownership, governance, and qualifications. Tax tracks classification, elections, filing groups, nexus, accounts, and returns. Differences can be valid, but unexplained differences create risk.

Key Reconciliation Fields

At least annually, compare legal name, EIN, state-law type, formation and dissolution dates, direct owner, federal tax classification, tax return filed, consolidated or combined group, fiscal year, responsible party, addresses, state accounts, payroll registrations, and foreign reporting obligations.

Common Mismatches

An LLC may be legally active but omitted from a tax schedule. An entity may be dissolved under state law while tax accounts remain open. Ownership may change legally before tax systems are updated. A name change may not reach all agencies. A single-member LLC may be incorrectly treated as a separate federal income-tax filer. These matters require professional analysis rather than assumptions.

Change Triggers

Formation, ownership transfer, conversion, merger, domestication, name change, responsible-party change, address change, election, and dissolution should trigger tax notification or review. The entity workflow should create tasks automatically or through a documented handoff.

Evidence and Confidentiality

Tax returns and personal tax identifiers may have narrower access than general entity records. The master register can record classification and responsible function without exposing full returns or personal data.

Governance and Timing

Tax elections and classifications may require governing approval, signatures, and deadlines. Preserve the advice, approval, filing evidence, and effective date. Do not assume that a state-law conversion produces the intended tax result.

> ***Control Point:*** *Legal status, tax status, and accounting status are separate fields. Each should have an owner and supporting evidence.*

Implementation Checklist

- Define shared legal-tax data fields.
- Perform scheduled reconciliation.
- Integrate change events with tax review.
- Resolve name, date, owner, and classification conflicts.
- Protect tax records and personal data.
- Preserve election and account-closure evidence.
- Report unresolved differences before transactions.

Key Takeaway

Tax and legal reconciliation ensures that the organization's formal structure and tax administration describe the same underlying reality.

CHAPTER 59.

International Subsidiary Governance

Additional Layers of Complexity

International entities introduce local corporate law, tax, accounting, employment, privacy, foreign investment, exchange-control, sanctions, language, notarization, legalization, and director-residency considerations. A U.S.-centered entity process should not be extended abroad without local advice.

Local Counsel and Corporate Secretarial Support

Define responsibility among internal legal, local counsel, corporate secretarial providers, tax, finance, and local management. The organization should know who maintains statutory registers, files annual returns, prepares local minutes, holds seals or original records, and monitors director or registered-office requirements.

Data Model

The global register should capture local legal form, jurisdiction, company number, registered office, directors, officers, shareholders, statutory auditor, fiscal year, tax identifiers, local counsel, filing calendar, ownership restrictions, and document language. Preserve both English translations and official-language records when appropriate.

Governance Calendar

International subsidiaries may require annual shareholder meetings, local board meetings, financial-statement approval, auditor appointment, beneficial-owner registers, capital maintenance, or local filings. Calendars should account for time zones, notarization, apostilles, translations, and original signatures.

Director Duties and Substance

Local directors may owe duties under local law and should receive complete materials. Tax or regulatory substance requirements may affect where meetings occur and who makes decisions. Avoid treating local directors as signature services without meaningful process.

Cross-Border Changes

Capital contributions, dividends, intercompany loans, guarantees, ownership transfers, and liquidations may require tax, foreign-exchange, investment, or regulatory approval. Build lead time and document source of funds and authority.

> ***Practice Note:*** *A global entity platform should support local detail without pretending that one country's terminology and workflow apply everywhere.*

Implementation Checklist

- Assign internal and local responsibility.
- Maintain official-language and translated records.
- Track local meetings, filings, and statutory registers.
- Confirm director, office, and substance requirements.
- Obtain cross-border tax and regulatory review.
- Protect personal data across jurisdictions.
- Audit local-provider records and access.

Key Takeaway

International governance requires a global control framework executed through informed local processes.

CHAPTER 60.

Board and Committee Calendar Management

Governance as a Recurring Program

Boards and committees require planned agendas, timely materials, accurate attendance, conflict review, minutes, action tracking, and follow-up. Entity management and corporate secretarial work intersect because decisions must be reflected in the permanent record.

Annual Calendar

Build a calendar based on bylaws, committee charters, financing covenants, regulatory requirements, strategic planning, budgets, financial reporting, officer elections, policy reviews, and recurring approvals. Reserve dates early and identify which matters require owner or shareholder action.

Agenda Development

Use a rolling agenda that distinguishes information, discussion, and decision items. Each decision item should identify the approving body, required threshold, supporting materials, presenter, conflicts, and proposed resolution.

Board Materials

Distribute materials through an approved secure channel with sufficient review time. Maintain version control and clearly identify late additions. Sensitive or privileged materials may require restricted access or separate handling.

Minutes and Action Items

Draft minutes promptly while facts are fresh. Track action items separately from the legal minutes so that operational detail does not obscure the official record. Approved minutes, consents, and exhibits should flow to the minute book.

Committee and Subsidiary Coordination

Committees may recommend but not finally approve certain actions. Subsidiary boards may require separate approvals even when the parent board has acted. The governance matrix should prevent assumptions that one approval covers all entities.

> ***Control Point:*** *Every agenda item seeking approval should identify the exact entity and decision-making body before materials are distributed.*

Implementation Checklist

- Create an annual governance calendar.
- Maintain a rolling agenda and decision log.
- Confirm authority and thresholds for each action.
- Distribute secure, version-controlled materials.
- Draft and approve minutes promptly.
- Track action items and unresolved conditions.
- File final records in each affected entity's minute book.

Key Takeaway

Board-calendar management turns governance from a series of urgent events into a predictable and well-documented operating rhythm.

CHAPTER 61.

Ethical Practice and Professional Judgment

Integrity of the Corporate Record

Entity professionals are often asked to move quickly, solve historical gaps, and satisfy transaction deadlines. The pressure can create requests to backdate documents, omit inconvenient facts, use a person's signature without clear authority, or characterize incomplete work as finished. Professional judgment begins with protecting the accuracy of the record.

Accuracy and Candor

Do not knowingly create, file, certify, or circulate false information. If a record is incomplete, label it accurately. If a filing was late, preserve the real dates. If approval is missing, escalate rather than reconstructing a misleading chronology.

Unauthorized Practice and Scope

Nonlawyer professionals should understand the boundary between process execution and legal advice. They can gather facts, prepare drafts under supervision, manage workflows, and identify issues. Legal conclusions, interpretation of law, and advice to clients or the organization should be handled by authorized counsel as required.

Confidentiality and Privilege

Protect confidential and privileged information, but do not assume that every communication with legal is privileged. Limit distribution to those with a need to know. Use approved systems and avoid discussing sensitive matters in public or insecure channels.

Conflicts and Personal Data

Disclose conflicts of interest and avoid using entity information for personal benefit. Handle personal identifiers, ownership data, and signatures with care. Verify identities when requests could facilitate fraud.

Speaking Up

The program should give professionals a safe escalation path for suspected fraud, sanctions concerns, bribery, falsified records, unauthorized transactions, discrimination, retaliation, or other misconduct. Document facts and follow policy.

> ***Practice Note:*** *The most important sentence in entity management may be, "I cannot complete this accurately without additional approval or information."*

Implementation Checklist

- Preserve true dates and complete evidence.
- Escalate requests to backdate or misstate facts.
- Understand professional scope and supervision.
- Protect confidentiality, privilege, and personal data.
- Verify authority and identity for sensitive changes.
- Disclose conflicts.
- Use established reporting and escalation channels.

Key Takeaway

Entity management depends on trust. Accuracy, candor, confidentiality, and appropriate escalation are nonnegotiable controls.

CHAPTER 62.

Audits, Internal Controls, and Assurance

Moving From Completion to Assurance

A process can appear complete while containing hidden errors. Assurance activities test whether controls are designed appropriately and operate consistently. They help legal leadership, internal audit, finance, and business executives rely on entity data and compliance reporting.

Control Design

For each material risk, define the control objective, frequency, owner, evidence, review method, and exception process. Examples include ensuring that every active entity has a valid registered agent, that ownership changes are supported by executed documents, and that annual filings are accepted before the deadline.

Testing Methods

Testing may include full-population reports, risk-based sampling, walkthroughs, document inspection, re-performance, user-access review, vendor reconciliation, and official-record comparison. Automated controls should be tested for configuration and exception handling.

Evidence Quality

Evidence should show who performed and reviewed the control, when it occurred, what population was considered, what exceptions were found, and how they were resolved. A screenshot without context may be insufficient.

Issue Rating

Rate findings based on legal consequence, financial exposure, transaction impact, duration, affected population, and likelihood. Distinguish isolated errors from systemic weaknesses. Assign management owners and deadlines.

Management Certification

Some organizations use periodic certifications from legal, tax, finance, and business owners confirming entity data, obligations, and open issues. Certifications should be based on documented review, not a general request to "confirm everything is correct."

Continuous Monitoring

Exception reports can provide ongoing assurance for missing registered agents, overdue tasks, invalid statuses, duplicate EINs, ownership totals, and records without evidence. Monitoring does not replace periodic independent review.

> ***Control Point:*** *A control that leaves no evidence cannot be reliably tested and should be redesigned.*

Implementation Checklist

- Map risks to control objectives.
- Document control owner, frequency, and evidence.
- Test design and operating effectiveness.
- Use risk-based sampling and full-population analytics.
- Rate and remediate findings.
- Validate closure independently.
- Report trends and systemic root causes.

Key Takeaway

Assurance gives stakeholders confidence that entity controls operate as designed, not merely that tasks appear complete.

CHAPTER 63.

Outside Counsel and Specialty Provider Management

When External Expertise Is Needed

Outside counsel and specialty providers may support formations, local law, complex governance, tax, securities, international subsidiaries, litigation, opinions, filings, searches, and transactions. Effective management requires clear scope, instructions, budget, authority, and knowledge transfer.

Matter Scoping

Provide the entity names, facts, jurisdiction, requested deliverable, legal question, deadline, internal owner, budget, and expected format. Identify whether advice should be reusable across the portfolio or limited to one matter. Avoid sending incomplete instructions that force providers to reconstruct basic facts.

Authority and Engagement

Confirm who may engage counsel, approve budget, direct work, and accept advice. Engagement letters should address scope, rates, staffing, confidentiality, conflicts, data security, records, and billing guidelines.

Work Allocation

Keep repeatable administrative work internal or with lower-cost providers when appropriate, while reserving counsel for legal analysis, complex drafting, negotiation, and high-risk matters. Standard forms and playbooks can reduce repeated legal research without replacing current review.

Billing Review

Invoices should identify the entity, matter, task, professional, time, rate, and expense. Review for scope, duplication, staffing, block billing, unsupported charges, and compliance with guidelines. Track estimates and communicate changes before overruns.

Knowledge Capture

Store final advice, filings, opinions, and templates in the approved repository with scope and date. Update procedures and training when advice changes the operating model. Do not allow important conclusions to remain only in an individual's inbox.

Performance

Evaluate responsiveness, expertise, practical judgment, diversity, budgeting, collaboration, technology, and outcomes. Use feedback in future assignments and panel decisions.

> ***Practice Note:*** *The best outside counsel relationship reduces future uncertainty by leaving the internal team with clear records, decisions, and reusable knowledge.*

Implementation Checklist

- Scope matters with complete facts and deliverables.
- Confirm engagement authority and budget.
- Allocate work to the appropriate resource level.
- Enforce billing and security guidelines.
- Preserve final advice and work product.
- Update internal procedures and data.
- Review performance and lessons learned.

Key Takeaway

External providers create the most value when their expertise is integrated into the organization's process, records, and future capability.

PART X

PRACTICAL TOOLKIT

Toolkit Introduction

The following templates are designed as vendor-neutral starting points. They should be adapted to the organization's law, governing documents, policies, technology, and approval structure. Bracketed fields indicate information to be completed. Each form should have an owner, version, approval date, and retention rule.

Template 1. Entity Formation Request

Field	Response
Request number	
Request date	
Requesting business unit	
Requestor and contact	
Business executive sponsor	
Requested completion date	
External deadline and consequence	

Proposed Entity

Field	Response
Proposed legal name - first choice	
Proposed legal name - alternatives	
Entity type	
Formation jurisdiction	
Principal business address	
Mailing address	
Business purpose	
Expected duration	
Domestic or international activities	

Ownership and Governance

Field	Response
Direct owner or owners	
Ownership percentages	
Ultimate parent	
Member-managed, manager-managed, or board-managed	
Proposed directors, managers, or general partners	
Proposed officers or authorized representatives	
Special voting or approval rights	

Operational Facts

☐ Will employ personnel.

☐ Will own or lease real estate.

☐ Will hold intellectual property.

☐ Will enter customer or vendor contracts.

☐ Will borrow money or grant liens.

☐ Will require bank accounts.

☐ Will require licenses or permits.

☐ Will operate in states other than the formation jurisdiction.

☐ Will involve non-U.S. owners, activities, or assets.

☐ Will be sold, financed, or transferred in a planned transaction.

Business Justification

Explain why a new entity is required and why an existing entity cannot serve the purpose:

____

____

____

____

Review and Approval

Function	Reviewer	Decision	Date	Conditions or Comments
Business				
Legal				
Tax				
Finance or Accounting				
Treasury				
Compliance or Licensing				
Insurance or Risk				

Template 2. Formation Approval Memorandum

To: [Approving Person or Body]

From: [Process Owner]

Date: [Date]

Re: Proposed Formation of [Legal Name]

Executive Summary

The requesting team seeks approval to form [entity type] in [jurisdiction] for the purpose of [purpose]. The entity is expected to be owned by [owner or owners] and managed by [management structure]. The requested effective date is [date].

Business Rationale

Describe the operational, contractual, financing, investment, tax, regulatory, or risk-management reason for forming the entity.

Proposed Structure

Item	Approved Design
Legal name	
Entity type	
Jurisdiction	
Direct owner	
Ultimate parent	
Management	
Initial officers or representatives	
Tax classification	
Registered-agent arrangement	
Principal activity and location	

Key Considerations

☐ Foreign qualification may be required in: ______________________________

☐ Licenses or permits may be required for: ______________________________

☐ Financing or investor requirements apply.

☐ Intercompany agreements will be required.

☐ Personal or sensitive information will be collected for tax or compliance purposes.

☐ Expedited filing is requested. Estimated additional cost: ____________

Approval Requested

Approval is requested to: (1) form the entity; (2) appoint the registered agent; (3) obtain an EIN; (4) prepare and execute organizational documents; (5) incur approved filing and service fees; and (6) complete required onboarding steps.

Approver	Signature or Approval Evidence	Date

Template 3. Jurisdiction Selection Worksheet

Factor	Jurisdiction A	Jurisdiction B	Jurisdiction C
Principal operations			
Employee locations			
Real property or facilities			
Investor or lender preference			
Governing law considerations			
Formation fee			
Annual report fee			
Franchise or privilege tax			
Registered-agent cost			
Expected foreign qualifications			
Public disclosure requirements			
Formation turnaround			
Certificate turnaround			
Regulated-industry requirements			
Tax considerations reviewed			
Exit or transaction considerations			

Recommendation:

____

Legal approval: ______________________ Date: __________

Tax approval: ______________________ Date: __________

Business approval: ______________________ Date: __________

Template 4. Name Review and Reservation Checklist

Proposed Entity Type: ______________________

Formation Jurisdiction: ______________________

Step	Complete	Evidence or Notes
Obtain at least three proposed names	[ ]	
Confirm required entity suffix	[ ]	
Search filing-office availability	[ ]	
Search internal entity register	[ ]	
Identify restricted or regulated words	[ ]	
Coordinate trademark review if required	[ ]	
Confirm domain or brand review if relevant	[ ]	
Reserve name if formation will be delayed	[ ]	
Track reservation expiration	[ ]	
Confirm final approved legal punctuation	[ ]	
Document trade or assumed names	[ ]	

Approved legal name: ______________________________

Approved by: ______________________________ Date: ______

Template 5. Formation and Onboarding Checklist

Task	Owner	Due Date	Complete	Evidence Location
Approve entity design			[]	
Confirm name availability			[]	
Appoint registered agent			[]	
File formation document			[]	
Confirm effective date			[]	
Record entity number			[]	
Obtain accepted filing			[]	
Create master-register record			[]	
Create digital minute book			[]	
Prepare governing document			[]	
Prepare initial consent or minutes			[]	
Appoint directors, managers, or officers			[]	
Document ownership issuance			[]	
Obtain EIN			[]	
Confirm tax classification			[]	
Establish accounting record			[]	
Open bank account			[]	
Establish signer authority			[]	
Confirm insurance			[]	
Complete licenses and permits			[]	
Assess foreign qualification			[]	
Add recurring obligations to calendar			[]	
Complete intercompany agreements			[]	
Notify business owner of readiness			[]	

Open conditions or exceptions:

Template 6. EIN and Tax Onboarding Intake

Entity Information

Field	Response
Exact legal name	
Trade name	
Formation jurisdiction	
Formation date	
Effective date	
Entity type under state law	
Principal business address	
Mailing address	
Principal activity	
Reason for applying	
Expected employees	
Accounting year end	

Responsible Party

Field	Restricted Response
Full legal name	
Title or relationship	
Basis for responsibility or control	
Taxpayer identification number received securely	[ ] Yes [ ] No
Identity verified under policy	[ ] Yes [ ] No

Tax Review

Item	Determination
Federal tax classification	
Election required	
State tax registrations	
Payroll registration	
Sales or use tax	
Special filing obligations	

Security Confirmation

☐ Personal information stored only in restricted systems.

☐ Confirmation notice stored in restricted entity record.

☐ Protected EIN field updated in master register.

Template 7. Initial Organizational Action Checklist

Action	Required	Approval Body	Complete	Document Reference
Adopt bylaws or operating agreement	[]		[]	
Elect or appoint directors	[]		[]	
Appoint managers	[]		[]	
Appoint officers	[]		[]	
Approve ownership issuance	[]		[]	
Accept capital contributions	[]		[]	
Establish fiscal year	[]		[]	
Approve EIN and tax elections	[]		[]	
Authorize bank accounts	[]		[]	
Authorize signers	[]		[]	
Approve intercompany agreements	[]		[]	
Ratify formation actions	[]		[]	
Approve material contracts	[]		[]	
Confirm registered agent	[]		[]	
Approve records location	[]		[]	

Prepared by: ______________________________ Date: ______________

Reviewed by: ______________________________ Date: ______________

Template 8. Master Entity Register Data Dictionary

Field Name	Definition	Format or Values	Source	Owner	Restricted?
Legal name	Exact current legal name	Text	Formation record	Legal	No
Prior legal name	Historical legal name	Text and effective dates	Amendment	Legal	No
Entity type	State-law legal form	Controlled list	Formation record	Legal	No
Domestic jurisdiction	Jurisdiction of formation	Controlled list	Formation record	Legal	No
Formation date	Date filed or created	YYYY-MM-DD	State record	Legal	No
Effective date	Legal effective date	YYYY-MM-DD	State record	Legal	No
Entity number	Filing-office identifier	Text	State record	Legal	No
Legal status	Current official status	Controlled list	Official source	Legal	No
Operational status	Internal lifecycle status	Controlled list	Business approval	Legal Ops	No
Direct owner	Immediate legal owner	Entity or person	Ownership record	Legal	Restricted
Ownership percentage	Legal or economic interest	Percentage or description	Ownership record	Legal	Restricted
Ultimate parent	Top controlling entity	Entity	Ownership chart	Legal	Restricted
Management structure	Board, manager, member, partner	Controlled list	Governing document	Legal	No
Officers or managers	Current roles with dates	Structured records	Consent or minutes	Legal	Restricted
EIN	Federal tax identifier	Protected text	IRS evidence	Tax	Yes
Tax classification	Federal tax treatment	Controlled list	Tax advice	Tax	Yes
Registered agent	Current agent	Provider or person	State record	Legal Ops	No
Annual obligation	Filing type and due rule	Structured task	Official guidance	Legal Ops	No
Document reference	Authoritative record location	Repository reference	Final document	Legal Ops	Restricted

Add organization-specific fields and validation rules before implementation.

Template 9. Annual Compliance Calendar Record

Field	Entry
Entity	
Jurisdiction	
Obligation type	
Period covered	
Legal due date	
Internal data deadline	
Internal approval deadline	
Target submission date	
Filing office	
Legal owner	
Tax or finance owner	
Business confirmer	
Required data	
Estimated government fee	
Estimated service fee	
Approval threshold	
Submission date	
Acceptance date	
Payment confirmation	
Evidence location	
Next due date	
Exceptions or notes	

Status Values: Upcoming; Data Requested; Under Review; Approved; Submitted; Rejected; Accepted; Evidence Stored; Closed.

Template 10. Foreign Qualification Analysis Questionnaire

Entity: ______________________________ **State Under Review:** ____________________

Activity	Yes	No	Details and Start Date
Office, facility, or regular physical location	[ ]	[ ]	
Employees or regular personnel	[ ]	[ ]	
Real property ownership or lease	[ ]	[ ]	
Recurring services performed in state	[ ]	[ ]	
Local project or construction activity	[ ]	[ ]	
State-specific license required	[ ]	[ ]	
Repeated customer contracts	[ ]	[ ]	
Material revenue or sales	[ ]	[ ]	
Inventory, equipment, or assets	[ ]	[ ]	
Bank account or financial relationship	[ ]	[ ]	
Litigation or isolated transaction only	[ ]	[ ]	
Expected duration			

Domestic status confirmed: [ ] Yes [ ] No

Tax, payroll, and licensing teams consulted: [ ] Yes [ ] No

Counsel determination: [ ] Qualify [ ] Do not qualify [ ] More facts required

Reasoning and conditions:

____
____

Template 11. Service of Process and Legal Notice Log

Field	Entry
Date and time received by registered agent	
Date and time received internally	
Entity served	
Jurisdiction	
Court, agency, or sender	
Matter caption or reference	
Document type	
Method of service	
Response or appearance deadline	
Internal recipients	
Outside counsel	
Insurance notice required	[ ] Yes [ ] No
Acknowledgment time	
Matter number	
Action owner	
Status	
Final disposition	
Evidence location	

Immediate Escalation Checklist

☐ Full document and envelope or delivery record preserved.

☐ Deadline independently calculated or confirmed.

☐ Litigation or subject-matter counsel notified.

☐ Business and risk stakeholders notified as required.

☐ Insurance notification assessed.

☐ Acknowledgment received from responsible attorney.

Template 12. Certificate and Official Document Request

Field	Response
Requestor	
Matter or transaction	
Entity legal name	
Jurisdiction	
Entity number	
Document requested	
Certificate of status or good standing	[ ]
Certified formation document	[ ]
Certified amendment or merger	[ ]
Complete filing history	[ ]
Apostille or authentication	[ ]
Required issue-date recency	
Required delivery format	
Deadline	
Expedited service approved	[ ]
Current status verified	[ ]
Order date	
Receipt date	
Evidence location	

Special instructions from receiving party:

____

____

Template 13. Officer, Director, Manager, or Member Change Form

Field	Response
Entity	
Role type	
Person leaving or changing role	
Resignation, removal, expiration, or transfer	
Effective date	
Successor	
New title or role	
Required approving body	
Governing-document provision	
Public filing required	[ ] Yes [ ] No
License notice required	[ ] Yes [ ] No
Bank or signer update required	[ ] Yes [ ] No
Power of attorney affected	[ ] Yes [ ] No
System access removal or change	[ ] Yes [ ] No
Contract notice required	[ ] Yes [ ] No

Supporting Documents

☐ Resignation or removal evidence

☐ Appointment or election consent

☐ Acceptance or joinder

☐ Updated incumbency or authority certificate

☐ Public or regulatory filing

☐ Updated register and organizational chart

Template 14. Ownership Change Checklist

Step	Owner	Complete	Evidence
Confirm current ownership		[]	
Review transfer restrictions		[]	
Identify consent and approval requirements		[]	
Confirm lender, investor, or regulatory consents		[]	
Prepare transfer or issuance documents		[]	
Confirm consideration or contribution		[]	
Satisfy conditions precedent		[]	
Admit new member or shareholder if required		[]	
Update ledger or ownership schedule		[]	
Update organizational chart		[]	
Notify tax and accounting		[]	
Reassess beneficial-ownership obligations		[]	
Review license and permit impact		[]	
Preserve pre- and post-closing records		[]	

Effective ownership after transaction:

Owner	Interest Type	Percentage or Rights	Effective Date

Template 15. Governance Action Request

Entity: ____

Requested Action: ______________________________________

Requested Effective Date: _________________________________

Business Purpose

____

____

Proposed Approval

Item	Response
Approving body	
Voting threshold	
Meeting or written consent	
Conflicts or related parties	
Required notices or waivers	
Supporting agreements	
Signatories	
External deadline	

Documents Attached

☐ Transaction agreement

☐ Financial or business summary

☐ Tax analysis

☐ Conflict disclosure

☐ Draft resolutions

☐ Governing-document excerpts

☐ Other: ______________________________

Completion Record

Step	Date	Owner	Evidence
Draft completed			

Step	Date	Owner	Evidence
Legal review			
Approval obtained			
Execution completed			
Register updated			
Minute book updated			

Template 16. UCC, Lien, Judgment, and Litigation Search Request

Field	Response
Matter or transaction	
Entity exact legal name	
Former names	
Entity type	
Formation jurisdiction	
Entity number	
Principal locations	
Search-through date required	
Deadline	

Search Scope

☐ UCC central filing office

☐ UCC local filing office

☐ Federal tax liens

☐ State tax liens

☐ Judgment liens

☐ Federal court litigation

☐ State court litigation

☐ Bankruptcy

☐ Real-property records

☐ Other: ________________________________

Instructions

☐ Include name variations identified by counsel.

☐ Provide copies of underlying filings.

☐ Include continuations, amendments, assignments, and terminations.

☐ Identify search limitations and index dates.

Reviewer and disposition: ____

Template 17. Entity Due Diligence Checklist

Category	Complete	Exceptions or Missing Items
Entity population confirmed	[ ]	
Formation document	[ ]	
All amendments and structural filings	[ ]	
Current governing document	[ ]	
Historical governing documents	[ ]	
Ownership ledger and supporting documents	[ ]	
Current organizational chart	[ ]	
Director, officer, manager, or partner records	[ ]	
Material consents and minutes	[ ]	
Domestic good standing	[ ]	
Foreign qualifications and good standing	[ ]	
Assumed names	[ ]	
Licenses and permits	[ ]	
EIN and tax classification confirmed	[ ]	
Registered-agent coverage	[ ]	
UCC and lien searches	[ ]	
Litigation and service-of-process review	[ ]	
Intercompany agreements	[ ]	
Financing restrictions	[ ]	
Dissolution or predecessor records	[ ]	

Material exceptions and remediation plan:

____

____

Template 18. Transaction Closing Entity Checklist

Deliverable	Responsible Party	Due	Status	Final Evidence
Entity population				
Good-standing certificates				
Certified formation documents				
Governing documents				
Ownership chart				
Board, member, or shareholder approvals				
Incumbency certificate				
Secretary or officer certificate				
Signature packets				
UCC searches				
UCC filing authorization				
Payoff and lien-release documents				
Legal opinion support				
Bring-down certificates				
Post-closing filings				
Final closing set				
Register and minute-book updates				

Open post-closing items:

____

____

Template 19. Dissolution Approval Memorandum

Entity: ________________________________

Requested by: __________________________

Proposed Dissolution Date: ____________

Reason for Dissolution

☐ Project or business abandoned

☐ Asset or entity sold

☐ Merger or reorganization

☐ Duplicate or unnecessary entity

☐ End of joint venture

☐ Other: ____________________________

Confirmation of No Remaining Need

Item	Owner	Confirmed	Notes
Assets transferred or disposed		[ ]	
Contracts terminated or assigned		[ ]	
Debt and liabilities resolved		[ ]	
Employees and benefits addressed		[ ]	
Tax plan approved		[ ]	
Bank accounts addressed		[ ]	
Licenses and permits addressed		[ ]	
Insurance reviewed		[ ]	
Litigation and claims reviewed		[ ]	
Foreign qualifications identified		[ ]	
Records custodian identified		[ ]	

Approval Requested

Approval is requested to commence wind-down, complete withdrawals, make required final filings and payments, distribute remaining assets as authorized, and file the domestic dissolution or cancellation when all conditions are satisfied.

Approver	Approval	Date	Conditions
Business			
Legal			
Tax			
Finance			
Treasury			

Template 20. Wind-Down and Dissolution Checklist

Task	Owner	Due	Complete	Evidence
Approvals obtained			[ ]	
Operations ceased			[ ]	
Employees addressed			[ ]	
Contracts terminated or assigned			[ ]	
Assets transferred or distributed			[ ]	
Liabilities and creditors addressed			[ ]	
Intercompany balances settled			[ ]	
Bank accounts closed			[ ]	
Insurance and bonds closed or continued			[ ]	
Licenses surrendered or transferred			[ ]	
Tax returns and clearances completed			[ ]	
Foreign withdrawals completed			[ ]	
Registered-agent plan completed			[ ]	
Domestic dissolution filed			[ ]	
Acceptance evidence stored			[ ]	
Final minute book assembled			[ ]	
Records custodian assigned			[ ]	
Register and calendar updated			[ ]	

Survival obligations:

____

____

Template 21. Vendor Evaluation Scorecard

Rate each category from 1 - Unsatisfactory to 5 - Excellent.

Category	Weight	Score	Weighted Result	Notes
Filing accuracy	15%			
Service-of-process speed	15%			
Geographic coverage	10%			
Portal usability	5%			
Reporting and data export	10%			
Information security	15%			
Invoice transparency	10%			
Account support	5%			
Integration capability	5%			
Business continuity	5%			
Contract and exit terms	5%			

Critical Issues:

☐ Security incident

☐ Missed service of process

☐ Repeated rejected filings

☐ Unreconciled invoice errors

☐ Inadequate data export

Recommendation: [ ] Renew [ ] Remediate [ ] Competitive Review [ ] Transition

Template 22. Invoice and Credit Card Reconciliation Log

Date	Vendor	Entity	Jurisdiction	Service	Government Fee	Service Fee

Date	Rush Fee	Total	Requestor	Receipt Stored	Accounting Code

Monthly Review

☐ Every charge matched to an approved request.

☐ Government and service fees separated.

☐ Duplicate charges investigated.

☐ Inactive and sold entities reviewed.

☐ Rush fees supported by approval.

☐ Receipts and acceptance evidence stored.

☐ Accounting coding confirmed.

Reviewer: ______________________________

Date: ______________

Template 23. Entity Management KPI Dashboard

Metric	Definition	Current Period	Prior Period	Target	Trend	Action
Active entities	Legally active entities in scope					
On-time filing rate	Accepted by legal due date					
Rejection rate	Rejected submissions divided by submissions					
Entities not in good standing	Official status exception					
Missing core documents	Entities missing required records					
Formation cycle time	Approval to accepted filing					
Certificate cycle time	Request to delivery					
Service routing time	Internal receipt minus agent receipt					
Open remediation items	Findings not closed					
Vendor invoice variance	Disputed or corrected charges					
Penalties and late fees	Avoidable compliance cost					
Data completeness	Required populated and verified fields					

Top Risks Requiring Decision:

1. ____
   ____
2. ____
   ____
3. ____
   ____

Template 24. Entity Health Audit Worksheet

Entity: ______________________ Audit Date: ______

Audit Area	Status	Evidence	Finding	Severity	Owner
Domestic status					
Foreign qualifications					
Registered agent					
Formation and amendments					
Governing documents					
Ownership and capitalization					
Directors, managers, and officers					
Annual reports and taxes					
Licenses and permits					
Assumed names					
EIN and tax classification					
Intercompany agreements					
Service-of-process records					
Transaction restrictions					
Minute-book completeness					

Severity Definitions: Critical; High; Moderate; Low; Administrative.

Remediation approval: ______________________

Template 25. Data Remediation Plan

Finding ID	Owner	Due Date	Validation Method	Closed Date

Closure Criteria

☐ Required approval obtained.

☐ Corrective document executed or filing accepted.

☐ Official status verified.

☐ Master register updated.

☐ Minute book updated.

☐ Downstream systems reconciled.

☐ Preventive control implemented.

☐ Closure independently validated.

Template 26. Records Retention Schedule - Entity Categories

Record Category	Suggested Treatment Subject to Counsel Review	Owner	Security	Trigger
Formation and amendments	Permanent or long-term	Legal	Confidential	Formation or filing date
Governing documents	Permanent or long-term	Legal	Confidential	Effective date
Ownership ledgers and transfers	Permanent or long-term	Legal	Restricted	Transaction date
Minutes and written consents	Permanent or long-term	Legal	Confidential	Approval date
Tax identification records	Per tax and legal schedule	Tax	Restricted	Filing or issuance date
Annual reports and receipts	Defined years after superseded	Legal Ops	Internal	Filing date
Good-standing certificates	Transaction or defined period	Legal Ops	Internal	Issue date
Registered-agent notices	Matter-based retention	Legal	Confidential	Receipt date
Service of process	Litigation hold or matter schedule	Litigation	Restricted	Receipt date
Licenses and permits	Life plus defined period	Business and Legal	Internal	Expiration or surrender
Draft governance documents	Short period unless material	Legal	Confidential	Final execution
Vendor invoices	Finance schedule	Finance	Internal	Payment date
Dissolution records	Permanent or long-term	Legal	Confidential	Dissolution date

Important: Apply legal holds before destruction and confirm jurisdiction-specific requirements.

Template 27. Digital Minute Book and Naming Standard

Folder Structure

1. 01 - Formation and State Filings
2. 02 - Governing Documents
3. 03 - Organizational Actions
4. 04 - Ownership and Capitalization
5. 05 - Directors, Officers, Managers, and Members
6. 06 - Consents and Minutes
7. 07 - Tax and Identification
8. 08 - Qualifications and Assumed Names
9. 09 - Annual Compliance and Certificates
10. 10 - Licenses and Permits
11. 11 - Registered Agent and Service of Process
12. 12 - Financing and Transactions
13. 13 - Intercompany Agreements
14. 14 - Amendments and Reorganizations
15. 15 - Dissolution or Divestiture
16. 99 - Superseded and Historical

File Naming Pattern

Legal Entity Name - Document Type - YYYY-MM-DD - Status

Status Terms

Draft; Under Review; Approved; Executed; Filed; Accepted; Certified; Superseded; Canceled.

Quality Checklist

☐ Exact legal name used.

☐ Date reflects effective, approval, filing, or issue date as defined.

☐ Final document is complete and legible.

☐ Signature pages and exhibits are included.

☐ Drafts are not stored as final records.

☐ Superseded versions are retained and labeled.

☐ Restricted documents have appropriate permissions.

Template 28. Entity Management RACI Matrix

Use R for Responsible, A for Accountable, C for Consulted, and I for Informed.

Core Legal and Finance Roles

Process	Legal Ops	Legal Counsel	Tax	Finance	Treasury
Formation intake					
Entity design					
Formation filing					
EIN application					
Governing documents					
Ownership change					
Annual filings					
Franchise taxes					
Foreign qualification					
Transaction diligence					
Dissolution					

Business and Control Roles

Process	Business	Compliance	Human Resources	IT Security
Formation intake				
Entity design				
Licenses				
Service of process				
Bank authority				
Ownership change				
Transaction diligence				
Dissolution				
Records retention				
System security				

Template 29. Standard Operating Procedure Framework

1. Document Control

Field	Entry
Procedure title	
Process owner	
Approver	
Version	
Effective date	
Next review date	
Supersedes	

2. Purpose

State the outcome and risk the procedure addresses.

3. Scope

Define entities, jurisdictions, teams, systems, and exclusions.

4. Definitions

Define specialized terms and statuses.

5. Roles and Decision Rights

Identify requestor, preparer, reviewer, approver, payer, record owner, and escalation contact.

6. Prerequisites and Required Inputs

List data, documents, approvals, and system access required before work begins.

7. Procedure

For each step state: action, owner, system, control, evidence, and expected timing.

8. Exceptions and Escalation

Describe rejected filings, missing approvals, conflicts, urgent requests, suspected fraud, and missed deadlines.

9. Records and Retention

Identify the official record, naming standard, access, and retention rule.

10. Metrics and Quality Review

Define cycle time, error rate, overdue threshold, sampling, and reporting.

11. Revision History

Version	Date	Change	Author	Approver

Template 30. Ninety-Day Entity Management Program Launch

Days 1 - 30: Stabilize and Inventory

☐ Identify all known entity data sources.

☐ Create an interim master entity inventory.

☐ Confirm service-of-process routing and backups.

☐ Identify filings due within ninety days.

☐ Identify entities not in good standing.

☐ Secure sensitive records and remove obsolete access.

☐ Document critical vendors and contracts.

☐ Establish an intake channel and escalation contact.

Days 31 - 60: Standardize and Reconcile

☐ Approve a data dictionary and status definitions.

☐ Establish digital minute-book structure.

☐ Reconcile domestic and foreign status.

☐ Reconcile registered-agent coverage and invoices.

☐ Create a compliance calendar with owners.

☐ Prioritize missing governing and ownership records.

☐ Publish formation, change, and dissolution workflows.

Days 61 - 90: Control and Report

☐ Launch risk-based entity health audits.

☐ Implement monthly dashboard and escalation reporting.

☐ Establish vendor scorecards and budget controls.

☐ Approve retention and sensitive-data procedures.

☐ Train business, finance, tax, and legal users.

☐ Create a twelve-month remediation and technology roadmap.

Executive Decisions Required:

1. ____ ____________________

2. ____ ____________________

3. ____ ____________________

PART XI

GLOSSARY, REFERENCE FRAMEWORKS, AND PROFESSIONAL PRACTICE

Glossary of Entity Management Terms

A

Acceptance Evidence. Official confirmation that a filing, registration, or order was accepted by the issuing authority. A payment receipt alone may not prove acceptance.

Administrative Dissolution. Loss or suspension of an entity's active status by a governmental authority, often for failure to file reports or pay required fees. It is different from a planned voluntary dissolution.

Affiliate. An entity or person related through direct or indirect ownership or control. The exact definition may vary by agreement or law.

Amendment. A document or action that changes an existing formation document, governing document, filing, or agreement.

Annual Report. A periodic filing required by a jurisdiction to update or confirm entity information. Some jurisdictions use terms such as statement of information, annual registration, or biennial report.

Apostille. A certificate used to authenticate the origin of certain public documents for use in another country under the applicable international framework.

Articles. A common term for public formation documents, such as articles of incorporation, organization, formation, dissolution, or amendment.

Assumed Name. A name under which an entity conducts business that differs from its legal name. Also called a fictitious name, trade name, or doing-business-as name.

Audit Trail. A chronological record showing who created, changed, approved, filed, or accessed data or documents.

Authorized Shares. The maximum number and classes of shares a corporation is permitted to issue under its charter, subject to amendment and applicable law.

Authorized Signer. A person with documented authority to sign specified documents or conduct specified transactions on behalf of an entity.

B

Beneficial Owner. A person who ultimately owns, controls, or benefits from an entity or asset under the definition applicable to a particular law, financial institution, or transaction.

Biennial Report. A periodic entity filing required every two years in some jurisdictions.

Board of Directors. The governing body of a corporation, generally responsible for oversight and major decisions subject to law, charter, bylaws, and shareholder rights.

Board Resolution. A formal decision adopted by a board of directors.

Business License. Authorization from a governmental or regulatory authority to conduct a specified activity, often in a particular location.

Bylaws. Internal governance rules of a corporation addressing matters such as meetings, voting, directors, officers, and procedures.

C

Cancellation. A filing or legal event that terminates certain entity types, registrations, or instruments. Terminology varies by jurisdiction.

Capital Account. An accounting and tax record associated with an owner's economic interest, particularly in partnerships and LLCs taxed as partnerships.

Capital Contribution. Cash, property, services, or other value contributed to an entity by an owner, subject to governing documents and law.

Cap Table. A capitalization table showing ownership interests, classes, quantities, rights, and related information. It should reconcile to legal issuance and transfer records.

Certificate of Authority. A document or status indicating that an out-of-state entity is authorized to conduct business in a jurisdiction. The term may also have other regulatory meanings.

Certificate of Conversion. A public filing used in some jurisdictions to change an entity from one legal form to another.

Certificate of Dissolution. A public filing used to terminate or begin termination of an entity, depending on jurisdiction.

Certificate of Existence. An official status certificate similar to a certificate of good standing. Terminology and content vary.

Certificate of Formation. A public document that creates an entity in some jurisdictions, commonly used for LLCs.

Certificate of Good Standing. An official statement concerning an entity's compliance or status under the records of an issuing authority.

Certificate of Incorporation. A public formation document for a corporation in some jurisdictions.

Certified Copy. A copy of an official document authenticated by the issuing authority as a true copy of its record.

Charter. A general term for a corporation's formation document and amendments.

Closing Binder or Closing Set. An organized collection of final transaction documents and evidence.

Compliance Calendar. A controlled schedule of legal, tax, license, governance, and other obligations with owners and due dates.

Consent. Approval given by a person or governing body. A written consent may permit action without a meeting when authorized.

Conversion. A statutory process changing an entity from one legal type to another while preserving continuity where permitted.

Corporate Separateness. The legal and operational distinction among entities and their owners or affiliates.

Corporation. A legal entity generally governed by shareholders, directors, and officers under applicable corporate law.

CP Notice or EIN Confirmation. An IRS communication confirming assignment of an Employer Identification Number. The specific notice type may vary.

D

Data Dictionary. A controlled description of each data field, including its definition, format, permitted values, source, owner, and validation rule.

Delayed Effective Date. A future date specified for a filing or transaction to become legally effective where permitted.

Direct Owner. The person or entity that immediately holds an ownership interest in another entity.

Director. A member of a corporation's board of directors.

Disregarded Entity. An entity treated as not separate from its owner for specified federal tax purposes, even though it remains a separate entity under state law.

Dissolution. The legal process of ending an entity's existence or beginning its winding up, depending on jurisdiction and entity type.

Distribution. A transfer of cash, property, or value from an entity to an owner in that capacity.

Doing Business. A legal concept used to determine whether an entity must register or qualify in a jurisdiction. The definition varies and is fact-specific.

Domestic Entity. An entity considered domestic in the jurisdiction under whose law it was formed.

Domestication. A statutory process that changes an entity's jurisdiction of organization while preserving continuity where permitted.

E

Effective Date. The date on which a filing, agreement, appointment, ownership change, or other legal event becomes operative.

Electronic Signature. An electronic sound, symbol, or process associated with a record and executed or adopted with intent to sign, subject to applicable law and policy.

Employer Identification Number. A nine-digit federal tax identification number assigned by the Internal Revenue Service to entities and other taxpayers for tax administration.

Entity. A legally recognized organization or structure, such as a corporation, LLC, partnership, or nonprofit corporation.

Entity Health Audit. A structured review of legal status, records, ownership, authority, compliance, and data quality.

Entity Management Platform. Software used to maintain entity data, documents, compliance tasks, ownership, and reports.

Entity Number. An identifier assigned by a filing or regulatory authority.

Equity Interest. An ownership interest in an entity, such as shares, membership interests, or partnership interests.

Escalation. Formal routing of an issue to a person with authority or expertise to decide or respond.

Evidence Location. The approved repository reference showing where the authoritative record of completion is stored.

F

Fictitious Name. A name used by an entity other than its legal name, subject to applicable registration requirements.

Fiduciary Duty. A legal duty that may apply to directors, officers, managers, partners, trustees, or others depending on role, law, and governing documents.

Filing Date. The date a filing office receives or records a document. It may differ from the legal effective date.

Filing Office. A governmental office that receives and maintains entity, UCC, license, or other official records.

Foreign Entity. In state entity law, an entity formed under another jurisdiction's law. The term does not necessarily mean non-U.S.

Foreign Qualification. Registration of an entity to conduct business in a jurisdiction other than its formation jurisdiction.

Formation Document. The public record filed to create an entity, such as articles or a certificate of formation or incorporation.

Franchise Tax. A tax or fee imposed by some jurisdictions for the privilege of being organized or doing business there. It may not be based on a franchise relationship.

G

General Partner. A partner with management authority and potential liability as provided by law and agreement in a partnership or limited partnership.

Good Standing. A status indicating compliance with specified requirements of an issuing authority. The scope varies and may not address tax, license, or all legal obligations.

Governing Body. The person or group with authority to make decisions for an entity, such as a board, members, managers, partners, or trustees.

Governing Document. An internal document establishing governance and economic rules, such as bylaws, an operating agreement, or a partnership agreement.

Governance Matrix. A summary of approval bodies, voting thresholds, reserved powers, and decision rights.

H

Holding Company. An entity formed primarily to own interests in other entities or assets.

I

Inactive Entity. An internal operational description that does not necessarily mean the entity has been legally dissolved or has no obligations.

Incumbency Certificate. A certificate identifying current officers, directors, managers, or authorized representatives, often used in transactions.

Independent Director or Manager. A person appointed under specified criteria, often in financing structures, whose approval may be required for certain actions.

Initial Report. A filing required by some jurisdictions shortly after formation or qualification.

Intercompany Agreement. An agreement between entities under common control documenting services, loans, licenses, leases, allocations, or other relationships.

Internal Deadline. An organization-imposed due date preceding the legal deadline to permit review, approval, submission, and correction.

Issued Shares. Shares that a corporation has actually issued from its authorized capital.

J

Joint Venture. A business arrangement in which parties share ownership, control, economics, or risk, often through a separate entity.

Jurisdiction. A state, country, tribal authority, locality, or other legal territory with authority over an entity or activity.

K

Know Your Customer or Customer Due Diligence. Processes used by financial institutions and other organizations to verify customers, ownership, control, and risk.

L

Legal Hold. A directive suspending ordinary destruction of records relevant to litigation, investigation, audit, or another preservation duty.

Legal Name. The exact name of an entity shown in its current official formation and amendment records.

Legal Opinion. A formal opinion of counsel addressing specified legal matters in a transaction.

Legal Operations. The discipline of managing legal work through process, technology, data, finance, vendors, and organizational design.

License. Governmental or regulatory authorization to engage in an activity, profession, or business.

Lien. A claim or security interest against property, arising by agreement, statute, judgment, or other law.

Limited Liability Company. A state-law entity commonly governed by members, managers, and an operating agreement.

Limited Partner. A partner whose role and liability are governed by the limited partnership agreement and applicable law.

Limited Partnership. A partnership structure generally consisting of at least one general partner and one or more limited partners.

M

Manager. A person or entity with management authority in a manager-managed LLC or other structure.

Manager-Managed LLC. An LLC in which management authority is vested in one or more managers as provided by law and the operating agreement.

Managed Filing Service. A service in which a provider monitors or completes specified recurring entity filings, subject to agreed responsibilities.

Master Entity Register. The organization's authoritative structured dataset of legal entities, ownership, status, authority, obligations, and records.

Member. An owner of an LLC, subject to the rights and obligations established by law and the operating agreement.

Member-Managed LLC. An LLC in which management authority is held by members as provided by law and the operating agreement.

Merger. A statutory transaction combining entities, with one or more surviving or resulting entities as provided by law and the plan of merger.

Minute Book. The organized official record of an entity's formation, governing documents, ownership, approvals, and material actions.

Minutes. The official record of a meeting's procedural facts and actions.

N

Name Reservation. A temporary filing that reserves an available entity name for a defined period where permitted.

Nonprofit Corporation. A corporation formed for nonprofit purposes under applicable law, which may separately seek tax-exempt status.

Notice Address. An address specified for contractual or legal notices. It may differ from the principal office or registered office.

O

Officer. A person appointed to an office of an entity, such as president, secretary, or treasurer, with authority defined by law, governing documents, resolutions, or delegation.

Operating Agreement. The principal internal governing agreement of an LLC.

Operational Status. An internal lifecycle classification, such as development, active, dormant, wind-down, or sold. It should be distinguished from legal status.

Organization Chart. A visual representation of ownership or reporting relationships. A legal organization chart should show legal ownership and effective dates.

Organizer. A person who signs or submits an LLC formation document, depending on jurisdiction. An organizer is not necessarily an owner or manager.

P

Parent Entity. An entity that owns or controls another entity directly or indirectly.

Partnership Agreement. The governing agreement of a partnership or limited partnership.

Permit. Governmental authorization for a particular activity, location, project, or condition.

Portfolio Rationalization. Review and elimination, merger, sale, or retention of entities based on current business need, risk, cost, and obligations.

Power of Attorney. A document authorizing a person to act for another within specified scope and duration.

Principal Office. The main business office identified under applicable law, filing, or internal policy. It may differ from the registered office.

Privilege Tax. A tax imposed by some jurisdictions on an entity's existence or business activity.

Professional Entity. An entity formed to provide professional services and subject to ownership, naming, or licensing restrictions.

Project Company. An entity formed to own, develop, finance, or operate a specific project or asset.

Q

Qualification. See Foreign Qualification.

Quorum. The minimum participation required for a governing body or owners to conduct business at a meeting.

R

RACI Matrix. A tool assigning who is Responsible, Accountable, Consulted, and Informed for a process.

Ratification. Approval or confirmation of a prior act, subject to applicable law and facts. It should not be confused with backdating.

Record Copy. The authoritative final version of a document retained under records policy.

Registered Agent. A person or entity designated to receive service of process and official notices for an entity in a jurisdiction.

Registered Office. The official address associated with the registered agent in a jurisdiction.

Registration Number. An identifier assigned by a filing, licensing, or regulatory authority.

Reinstatement. Restoration of an entity's active status after administrative dissolution, revocation, or similar loss of status, subject to applicable requirements.

Related-Party Transaction. A transaction involving an entity and a person or organization with a relationship that may create a conflict or special approval requirement.

Responsible Party. For EIN purposes, the person identified under current IRS instructions as ultimately owning or controlling the entity or exercising effective control, subject to applicable rules.

Restated Document. A document that consolidates an original document and amendments into a current form, sometimes with additional amendments.

Restricted Data. Information requiring the highest level of internal access control, such as taxpayer identification numbers or personal identification documents.

S

Secretary's Certificate. A certificate by an entity's secretary or other authorized person attaching or certifying governance records, incumbency, or authority.

Service of Process. Formal delivery of legal documents such as summonses, complaints, subpoenas, or notices under applicable law.

Shareholder. An owner of shares in a corporation.

Signature Authority. Legal or delegated power to sign or act for an entity within a defined scope.

Single-Member LLC. An LLC with one member. Its state-law form and federal tax classification are separate concepts.

Special-Purpose Entity. An entity created for a limited asset, project, financing, investment, or transaction purpose.

Standing Authority. Ongoing delegated authority to complete defined actions without obtaining separate approval each time.

Statement of Information. A periodic state filing updating entity information in some jurisdictions.

Stock Certificate. A physical or electronic certificate evidencing shares, subject to the corporation's records and applicable law.

Stock Ledger. The authoritative record of share issuances, ownership, transfers, cancellations, and related information.

Subsidiary. An entity owned or controlled directly or indirectly by another entity.

Successor Entity. An entity that succeeds to specified rights, assets, liabilities, or legal identity through a transaction or law.

T

Tax Classification. The treatment of an entity for tax purposes, which may differ from its state-law form.

Tax Clearance. Confirmation from a tax authority that specified tax requirements have been satisfied, sometimes required for withdrawal or dissolution.

Trade Name. A business name used in commerce that may differ from the legal entity name.

Transaction Closing. The point at which transaction documents become effective and required conditions are satisfied, often accompanied by funding or transfer.

Transfer Restriction. A legal or contractual limitation on transfer of ownership interests.

U

UCC Financing Statement. A public filing used to provide notice of a security interest under Article 9 of the Uniform Commercial Code.

Ultimate Parent. The highest entity in an ownership chain that is not controlled by another entity within the defined group.

Uniform Commercial Code. A body of state commercial law based on uniform provisions, including Article 9 on secured transactions.

V

Validation Rule. A requirement that data satisfy a defined format, value, relationship, or supporting-evidence condition.

Version Control. A process for identifying, managing, and preserving document versions and status.

Voluntary Dissolution. A dissolution initiated through authorized entity action rather than imposed administratively.

W

Wind-Down. The process of ceasing operations, resolving assets and liabilities, closing obligations, and preparing an entity for dissolution or sale.

Withdrawal. Formal termination of an entity's authority to conduct business as a foreign entity in a jurisdiction.

Written Consent. A written action adopted without a meeting by the required persons or governing body when permitted.

State and Jurisdiction Research Framework

Entity laws, fees, forms, taxes, and filing practices change. Rather than relying on a static list, maintain a jurisdiction research record that is reviewed before each formation, qualification, major change, or dissolution.

Research Category	Questions to Verify
Filing authority	Which office creates and maintains the entity record?
Entity types	Which structures are available and what terminology applies?
Name rules	What suffixes, restricted words, and distinguishability standards apply?
Formation	What document, signatures, addresses, and disclosures are required?
Effective date	Is delayed effectiveness permitted?
Registered agent	Who may serve and what address rules apply?
Initial report	Is a filing required shortly after formation or qualification?
Recurring report	Is the filing annual, biennial, or based on anniversary date?
Franchise or privilege tax	Which agency administers it and how is it calculated?
Public information	Which officers, managers, owners, or addresses are public?
Foreign qualification	What activities trigger review and what documents are required?
Good standing	Which obligations affect certificate availability?
Amendments	What approvals and filings apply to names, purposes, or capital?
Merger and conversion	Which statutory transactions are permitted?
Withdrawal	Are tax clearance, final reports, or agent consent required?
Dissolution	What approvals, notices, taxes, and filings apply?
Reinstatement	What cure period and documents apply after loss of status?
Processing	What standard and expedited options exist?
Records	Which evidence should be retained and for how long?

Selected Authorities and Further Reading

The following sources provide foundational or current guidance. Readers should consult the most recent editions, regulations, instructions, official forms, and jurisdiction-specific materials.

- Amazon Kindle Direct Publishing, paperback manuscript formatting and submission guidance.
- Internal Revenue Service, Instructions for Form SS-4, Application for Employer Identification Number.
- Internal Revenue Service, guidance on business structures, responsible parties, and changes to business address or responsible party.
- Financial Crimes Enforcement Network, current Beneficial Ownership Information reporting guidance and regulations.
- Uniform Law Commission, Uniform Electronic Transactions Act.
- Electronic Signatures in Global and National Commerce Act, 15 U.S.C. sections 7001 and following.
- Uniform Commercial Code, Article 9, as enacted in the relevant jurisdiction.
- Model Business Corporation Act and official comments.
- Revised Uniform Limited Liability Company Act and official comments.
- Revised Uniform Limited Partnership Act and official comments.
- Official business-entity statutes, regulations, forms, and instructions of each applicable jurisdiction.
- Official tax, licensing, labor, securities, charitable-registration, and industry-regulatory guidance applicable to the entity's activities.

Closing Perspective

Entity management is quiet infrastructure. When it works, the organization can form, finance, operate, acquire, sell, and close entities with confidence. When it fails, the consequences surface at the worst possible time: a transaction, lawsuit, audit, tax deadline, leadership change, or regulatory inquiry.

The discipline is built through ordinary actions performed consistently. Verify the legal name. Document the approval. Preserve the executed record. Update the register. Monitor the deadline. Reconcile the vendor. Protect the data. Escalate the exception. Close the loop.

The strongest legal operations teams do more than maintain entities. They create institutional trust in the organization's legal structure. That trust allows business leaders to move faster because they know the records are reliable, authority is documented, obligations are visible, and risk will be raised before it becomes a crisis.

About the Author

Iveliz Rivera is a legal operations and corporate governance professional with more than fifteen years of experience supporting in-house legal teams, law firms, corporate transactions, compliance programs, contract operations, entity portfolios, and renewable energy projects. Her work has included building entity-management processes, supporting project finance and asset transactions, coordinating outside counsel and vendors, developing legal operations systems, maintaining complex subsidiary portfolios, and improving governance and compliance workflows.

She wrote *The Legal Operations Guide to Entity Management* to provide a practical, vendor-neutral resource for professionals responsible for the legal structures that support modern organizations.

Entity Management Action Plan

Use this page to translate the guide into the next set of controlled improvements for your organization.

Priority	Current Risk or Gap	Action	Owner	Target Date	Closure Evidence
1					
2					
3					
4					
5					

Decisions Required From Leadership

1. ____ __________________

2. ____ __________________

3. ____ __________________

First Review Date

____

Success Measures

☐ Critical legal-status issues are resolved.

☐ Service-of-process routing is tested.

☐ Entity data is verified and reconciled.

☐ Upcoming compliance obligations have accountable owners.

☐ Core records are complete, secure, and searchable.

☐ Remediation progress is reported to leadership.

Notes

Notes

Notes

Notes

www.ingramcontent.com/pod-product-compliance
Lightning Source LLC
LaVergne TN
LVHW022209200926
848481LV00006B/1907